Chapmar
Hamish Henderson

CW00959862

ISBN 0 906772 68 0   ISSN 0308-2695   © *Chapman* 1995

CHAPMAN
4 Broughton Place, Edinburgh EH1 3RX, Scotland
Tel 0131–557 2207   Fax 0131–556 9565
Editor: Joy Hendry   **Associate Editor: Robert Calder**
Production: Peter Cudmore   Administration: Joy Hare
Volunteers: Harald Leusmann, Katie Lockwood, Heather Toye, Paul Trainer

Submissions:
Chapman welcomes submissions of poetry,
fiction and critical articles provided they are
accompanied by a stamped addressed envelope
or International Reply coupons

Subscriptions:

	Personal		Institutional	
	1 year	2 years	1 year	2 years
UK	£13	£25	£17	£30
Overseas	£17/$30	£30/$57	£21/$37	£39/$68

THE SCOTTISH **ARTS** COUNCIL

THE CITY OF EDINBURGH DISTRICT COUNCIL
EDINBURGH
IMPROVING SERVICES – CREATING JOBS

Printed by Mayfair Printers, Print House, William Street, Sunderland, Tyne & Wear

Editorial

With this issue we have to mark the death of two very important figures in the world of Scottish letters: Tom Scott and Michael Grieve, both men of inestimable courage, independence of mind, and, as the Scots expression goes, "caa through". Many people are simply not replaceable, having something special and unique to contribute to the rest of humanity, and these two were of that category.

Tom Scott leaves behind a very remarkable body of work, ranging from beautiful haunting lyrics to epic poems, some book-length like *The Tree*, celebrating the wonders of evolution, *The Dirty Business*, a diatribe on war. He could turn his poetic hand to almost any theme, and firmly believed that poetry could tackle anything, however difficult, technical or obscure. In this respect he took a lead from MacDiarmid, but was never in any way a disciple. Indeed, this commitment to the scope of poetry led him to grossly undervalue his own shorter, lyric poems which range from beautiful love lyrics to comic squibs, from poems like the perfect 'Villanelle de Noel' to the political attack on capitalism in 'Aberfan'.

His estimate of his own contribution was always essentially modest. He felt that he couldn't himself achieve the realisation of his own poetic vision, but hoped that he had pointed the way forward for other poets to do what he could not. In this, he was perhaps too reticent, but any assessment of his real poetic achievement will be impossible until the several long poems which remain unpublished or unfinished are published. There are also shorter poems, and quite a few early works which he had allowed to remain uncollected. It is tragic that he died while an application to the Scottish Arts Council for a bursary was in process to make this work possible given his failing health, and the work remains to be completed. But one thing is certain, he was a pioneer among poets.

Tom Scott, having led a quiet, reclusive life for many years, wasn't known on the reading circuit, despite having a wonderful rich speaking and singing voice. His work has suffered as a result, not being nearly widely enough known even here in Scotland. We have over the years regularly featured his work and copies of Chapman 47–8, with a special feature on his work, can still be obtained.

Being the son of a genius must be one of the most difficult roles to play, but Michael Grieve not only maintained that role with expert devotion, promoting and editing his father, Hugh MacDiarmid's work, but was very much his own man also. He has made an inestimable contribution to literature in Scotland, to journalism and to the development of the Scottish media, particularly via STV. He was behind STV's bold and comprehensive poetic archive programme in verse, which captured on television Scotland's best writers reading their work. Alas, Tom Scott was one of the few poets omitted. He was also a great friend and supporter of so many involved in the arts in Scotland, and showed enormous courage in coping with illness during his last years, never seeming to be daunted by it, but carrying on with indomitable cheerfulness.

Both men died in August, only a few days before this issue's copy date, so it hasn't been possible to do more than give their deaths this mention, but our sincere condolences go out to their family and friends, who will sharply feel the loss of these two unique spirits.

On a happier note, it is with great pleasure that we congratulate our Irish friend and colleague Seamus Heaney on winning this year's Nobel Prize for Literature. It is rare for that prize to come to these islands, and it is all the more welcome that the prize comes to one who bridges many cultural divides, and it fittingly crowns his well-deserved reputation as a major figure in world literature.

Tom Scott Remembered

Kathleen Raine

Tom Scott has been in my life for more than fifty years, so how is it possible to think of him as having ceased to be? Past, present or future, there is only NOW, and it has always been NOW where we have met.

I remember Tom first in London, before the war, where he was working as a postman and writing in English, tall, spare and singular. Later I met him at George and Paddy Fraser's gatherings of poets. Poetry in that circle, and at that time, was taken very professionally, as a craft, a skill to be mastered. Tom was a professional, a makar. Eliot was our mentor and judge and Tom Scott was one of the poets Eliot respected, because Tom respected language.

Tom had a beautiful voice that could have made him a professional singer. All the gifts traditionally found in Scotland's poets met in Tom: bard, singer, scholar, satirist and flyter, and impassioned defender of the dignity of man. But although a lifelong socialist, Tom's socialism had little to do with collective man: it is the dignity and pride of individual men that he both represented and honoured. His political gestures were not those of any party, but his own. It was characteristic of him that once when the Orange Order was marching through Edinburgh, Tom with his tall, gaunt form and his red beard, deliberately crossed the road through their ranks. I believe Tom would have been agin any government, would have seen it as the task of the poet at all ties to hold to values of which any government save that of the Holy City will fall short, and to proclaim no less. Scottish patriot as he was, he resigned even from the SNP! Politics for him was not 'the art of the possible' but a vision of the Kingdom in which each man and woman will stand – as Tom himself did – in he freedom and dignity of his own humanity. Proud as he was to be a son of the working class, his father, the stonemason celebrated in *Brand the Builder* was no product of the Industrial Revolution, but of the age-old tradition of skilled craftsmen, who knew stone, who had built Scotland's stone walls and broons, her castles and her abbeys, her good stone houses and her proud universities. Tom was heir to all these, as learned in his country's great heritage as any man in Scotland. Like everything else about him, his learning was his own, and his great work on the history of Scottish literature too controversial to be published finally by the Oxford University Press who commissioned it. Indeed a professor at Edinburgh University described Tom to me with considerable respect as one of the two most difficult men in Scotland – the other was my friend John Lorne Campbell, the Gaelic scholar, who had his own battles with the powers in the land.

After the Second World War Tom's opportunity to study came through Newbattle Abbey in the all too short golden age of its first Principal, Edwin Muir, who gathered about him a talented generation of Scottish poets. From Newbattle Tom went on to Edinburgh University where he gained the highest academic distinctions; but characteristically refused the proffered honour of Poet in Residence in protest at the absence of any school of Scots language and literature on the syllabus of any Scottish university. Again, he stood for no group or party, it was "the voice of the bard" that spoke, though at the cost of his own career in the University.

I believe 'The Ship', a long poem that takes the wreck of the Titanic as a metaphor for the end of our materialist civilisation, is the finest satiric poem of the century to be written in this island. The poem has the eloquence of John Knox striking fear into the hearts of his auditors, but also Tom's other side, his great tenderness and pity, his veneration for woman – as in the great 'Sea Dirge: A Mither Keenin'. Some of his lyrics are the equal of any Scottish poet in my generation, and I am proud to hae published a group of them in *Temenos*, a Review of the Arts of the Imagination which I edited. Love poetry too is an aspect of the genius of Scotland Tom so fully expressed in his work and in himself. And though he writes of it in no poem known to me, he loved to fish for salmon in Scotland's swift rivers. I remember being his guest to share a fine fish Tom had landed and Heather, his wife, prepared.

Tom was, above all, a master of language, in song or speech, lyric or satire. In his fine translations Villon's sonnets and Dante's *terza rima* seem native to lowland Scots, the language he enriched no less than MacDiarmid. His poems will continue to speak from their pages in that living voice of his, which will never be silent. For it is a strange law that works of genius, undervalued at the time because they are strange and strong, in time come to be recognised. Times change, and fashions, but the living truth of imagination remains, we recognise it in the end because it corresponds to our own deepest truth. With the publication in 1993 by *Chapman* and *Agenda* of Tom Scott's *Collected Shorter Poems* it is clear that his work has that immortal quality. We hope his longer poems, in all their variety from the sense of sheer wonder of *The Tree* to the loud pipe-music of the battlefield on which he delighted to wield his claymore will follow. What a harvest. How proud I am that I could call him friend.

C.M. Grieve

To those of my old school who fell in the Second World War

(from the Broughton High School magazine, 1946)

So, to-day; hope lies
In the free and many-sided spirit of humanity
Against one-man Domination.
Beyond the meaningless and dead splendours of Versailles,
The glowing beauty of Chartres
Speaks imperishably through the ages.
And even so will the future see you,
Little groups of comrades of my old School,
Who went out
Against the Powers and Principalities of Darkness.

Hail and farewell, my friends!
At the moment it seems
As if the pressure of a loving hand had gone,
The touch
Under which my close-pressed fingers seemed to thrill
And the skin divide up into little zones
Of heat and cold whose position continually changed
So that the whole of my mind, held in that clasp,
Was in a state of eternal movement.
My eyes – that were full of pride,
My hands – that were full of love,
Are empty again – for a while,
For a little while!

Norman Kreitman

On Board

The drowning man asks "Why, why?"
What he gets is a lesson in physics
on the sinking of bodies. The ship lurches on.

A cup skitters a tattoo
across the table, pictures thump
to the floor. Already the decks are gaping.

Those fortunate crew
not yet washed overboard are busy with brooms;
they need to look useful, find honour in chores.

For myself I think less
about this floundering hulk, its charts
long mislaid, the captain drunk or dead.

Instead I grow more aware
of the strange seas in which it wallows;
the sense of distance; the crying of gulls.

Illustration by Tasb MacLeod

Drama? You are mistaken. As always the sunlight
is a white sheet from here to the vineyards.
It blesses the grateful lizards, calms the breeze,
lights to jewels the quartz beads
twinkling in stone doorways – whether standing
or tumbled, for the street now resembles
a jaw of broken teeth. In gardens, as always,
stand poppy and hibiscus in a red duet,
where men with eyes of wolves last night
went looting among other flames.

This morning in the silent, deserted city
the bark of a protesting dog. Seldom
have I heard such quiet, as if silence spread
in wave on wave from a central stillness.
Then, faintly on the breeze, that sound of keening
as the women filed into the square.
The queen wept too, her clothes shockingly tattered.
She was perhaps already a slave;
I cannot say – events confuse when too suddenly
they remind me how things are.
The priests had blessed us, said that disaster
could not cross our proud walls.
And we listened, though we knew that the gods

are as fickle as our Aegean –
the long, flat calms which choke the summer
or autumn's deadly storms. Better
always to fear the sea, whatever its mood.

As I said, events have brought us nothing new,
only perhaps a sharpening of the air.
See, the smoke has cleared, and in a luminous sky
the carrion fowl again go round
their scripted circles. As for young Cassandra
who among us has never tasted outrage?·
We old men know how the wrong that is here,
or another like it, waits everywhere.
Yet those who remain, flotsom not worth the taking,
must bundle a pot into a cloak
and already dry-eyed, leave on these stones
a track of sticky, dark-brown footprints, and go.

February 1993

A daffodil at my door is about to stand up.
A stub of yellow on a crooked stem
     its face locked earthwards
breaks the Narcissus gaze, watches the world
forget its map and metamorphose
     to blueness called a sky.

But the freshness half-deceives; last March
the same bell lifted the same small quiet.
     A year has paced by
pulsing to the drumbeat of disaster,
with Bosnian faces wrecked with grief
     or lusting for tribal murder.

The TV shows the rim of a mountain, the snow
a shawl over head and shoulders,
     the stare of indifferent stone.
A house blooms in fire at the roadside
among tendrils of rusty wire. Lower, nearer,
     a huddle of daffodils.

Flowers do not console, and images mislead,
though Spring too is recurrent fact
     with its own slow beat
sometimes heard, and sometimes understood.
This year, against all the clamour of questions,
     I merely observe
     its silent, sly return.

Patrick Clark

Nightingales Die

Nightingales die. He was not born for Death.
Life cheated him, then Death came to destroy.
Sing your song, lad, and ease Death's dying breath.

Science sniffs: "You *will cling* to the myth."
"Songs may live on. Singers join Death's convoy."
Nightingales die. He was not born for Death.

Off-key, he sang of grace, a simpleton's faith
in Life that planned with Death to filch his joy.
Sing your song, lad, and ease Death's dying breath.

Enter Death's hexagon, one cruciform wreathe.
Song-silent, today, minstrel-boy?
Nightingales die. He was not born for Death.

Substance belies the silence here beneath.
Death said: "I'm the immortal. Life's my toy."
Sing your song, lad, and ease Death's dying breath.

Death, Life, he has soared beyond you both,
sings to a host of stars without annoy.
Nightingales die. He was not born for Death.
Sing your song, lad, and ease Death's dying breath.

The Blush

I long to follow where those blushes go,
revealed ambivalences of her blood,
graphing the progress of her yes and no.

O rare phenomenon, roses top to toe,
Eros alerted, Psyche waxing red.
I long to follow where those blushes go.

Did one quick flash of wit produce this show?
The double-entendre, episcopally lewd,
graphing the progress of her yes and no.

Rose of the world, root of the verb to know,
where the bee comes to lose his perfumed head,
graphing the progress of her yes and no.

Is this her blood's unwilling ebb and flow,
or rose-red blood cells willing what they would?
I long to follow where those blushes go,
graphing the progress of her yes and no.

Prince's Square

Young nineteen-ninety, epicene in blue jeans and earrings,
ascending and descending like gods from heaven,
in machines of glass and gold with conscious stares,
heighten our here in consciousness's haven.

Solemn stairs on chromium ball-bearings,
descend and ascend to heaven,
present egos with cool exteriors,
while a trio of coruscating, cool guitars
scatter their dazzling Aldebarans of jazz
among the young immortals' cool razzamatazz.

The Miracle

Weeding his earth, he trailed out
from their incense-rich root-run a bine
of buttercups, cleavers, couch-grass,
sweet, self-seeking tangle of green.

"The hem of his cloak", silence said,
echoing the woman who bled.
(How does light come in the head?)
Healed by a touch of the twill
bobbing at the Rabbi's heel.

And silence dove-thundered and
spoke to the green in its hand,
echoed again the old plea:
"May I be cured, Sir, of me?"

Billy Watt

Medusa in Clyde Square

Dji hear aboot it
seems shid been steyin
In this sorta convint

When sum heid bummer
Sea captn ur sumhm
Goes an rapes ur

Nixt thing his wife fines oot
Maims the lassie fur life
Face wurss thin the backia buss

Diz nuthinty him but
Aw naw
Seems she wis a fine-lookin lassie befoar

Naebdi wid lookit ur
Twice efter that
Then ti croon it aw

This this sykopath
Goes an slits ur throat
They found ur lyin

Wi a booatla white hoarse
Under the cranes
O Kindcaids yerd

Depressn intit
Furst the Gaffer rooins yi
The yir ain kind finish the joab

Mother

Your hands changed me when I was young,
swaddled away the bright green curd
that I made of your mother's milk;

and now I have to swab your mess
from the bathroom floor – this time not
just excrement but blood as well.

You were always there for me
(to much perhaps) yet now the knob
of your elbow is a budless graft.

– I can not make you help yourself –

I mistrust the new vehemence
with which you state how you can not
spend one more winter in this house,

can't coax your eye to consider
where the wind ripples on Whinhill
or clouds lour on Dumbarton rock.

When I have cleaned your mess and failed
again to make you help yourself,
I go back to my shadows there, shadows,

and sounds of creaking waterpipes,
high heels tapping overhead,
seagulls whirling like strident wraiths...

If this is love then it is not
what I expected it to be.

The grim sister

I I am grim sister to the stone
cool columns of this barren temple.
They all come here to look at me.
Let them: I am untouchable.
Like Lot's wife in reverse I come
upon their chalcedonic faces,
on postures petrified in flight:
those whose temerity I flushed
from the scratched bronze of a mirror
(dropped at the crucial moment)
or from the dark sump of a pool.
Terror is what they found here: terror
congealed in a sidelong glance.

II I know the textures of stones
better than a lapidarist,
have felt them in the loveless nights:
the seductive glide of marble,
groove and sass if rippled limestone,
pimpled basalt, blood-hot cinnabar.
The gentle scrape of soapstone.
Wandering in the sculpted shadows
I am accused by abrasive crusted ores.

III Brute reek in the pillared darkness,
clatter and heave of hooves
stamping down the votive grapes,
bitter olives. He opened me up
like a pomegranate
while the punitive sea swilled
drunkenly around Her altar.
This was my punishment for being
beautiful.

And now inside I feel
the fluttering beat of hooves always.

IV And hissing in my ears always:
which is my punishment for being
a victim.

My food tastes of pebbles.
At times I surprise myself
by finding rock crystal on my tongue
and not the expected blue fig.

Could none of these keen-eyed heroes
who hoped to evade their limitations
have stopped to consider the victim
left to patrol this rocky waste
chastised by snakes
and eating moonfruit?

St Columbia exorcises the well of the Scots

The beached curraghs cant on the sand
like turtle shells: empty vessels.
Colum, the renegade from Derry,
has sailed across the grey heave

and fall of heathen waters
to this well: tobar na h'oige.
His tonsured head allowed no place
for doubt to cling in the damp hard nights.

And the well? Its tender water
can open a door between two worlds,
can cure the red or yellow fever,
dissolve love, deflect the evil eye.

People keep their sullen distance
from the cowled monks with sea-bleached feet
and pinched faces. Yet they hunger
for new wonders, weary of the old.

Thin peat smoke coils up from squat huts
laced with dried fish, while the chipping
of stone can be heard on stone.
A sinus is cleared with a wet slap

then, while his monks kneel in the new way,
the tall man from over the water
invokes his god in a voice of iron –
then he cups his hands and drinks.

The flat water trembles, the leaves
whisper. Tattooed watchers move back
in silent unison—everyone
waiting for something to happen.

But nothing happens.

On the trembling membrane of water
pond-skaters move the filaments
of their legs. Overhead, branches
click, click, as hunting eyes peer out.

it is the end of one culture,
the beginning of another.

Coloured Lights

Leila Aboulela

I cried a little as the bus started to fill up with people in Charing Cross Road and passed the stone lions in Trafalgar Square. Not proper crying, with sobs and moans, but a few silly tears and water dribbling from my nose. It was not the West Indian conductor who checked my pass that day but a young boy who looked bored. The West Indian conductor is very friendly with me, he tells me I look like one of his daughters and that he wants one day to visit the Sudan, to see Africa for the first time. When I tell him of our bread queues and sugar coupons, he looks embarrassed and leaves me to collect the fares of other passengers. I was crying for Taha or maybe because I was homesick, not only for my daughters or my family but sick with longing for the heat, the sweat, and the water of the Nile. The English word 'homesick' is a good one, we do not have exactly the same word in Arabic. In Arabic my state would have been described as 'yearning for the homeland' or 'the sorrow of alienation', and there is also truth in this. I was alienated from this place where darkness descended unnaturally at 4pm and people went about their business as if nothing had happened.

I was in a country which Taha had never visited and yet his memory was closer to me than it had been for years. Perhaps it was my new solitude, perhaps he came to me in dreams I could not recall. Or was my mind reeling from the newness surrounding me? I was in London for a one-year contract with the BBC World Service. Each day as I read the news in Arabic my voice, cool and distant, reached my husband in Kuwait, and my parents who were looking after my daughters in Khartoum.

Now I was older than Taha had been when he died. At that time he was ten years older than me and like my other brothers he had humoured me and spoiled me. When he died, my mind bent a little and has never straightened since. How could a young mind absorb the sudden death of a brother on the day of his wedding? It seemed at first to be a ghastly mistake, but that was an illusion, a mirage. The Angel of Death makes no mistakes. He is a reliable servant who never fails to keep his appointment at the predetermined time and place. Taha had no premonition of his own death. He was fidgety, impatient, but not for that, not for the end coming so soon. It was too painful to think of what must have been his own shock, his own useless struggle against the inevitable. Nor did anyone else have foreknowledge. How could we when we were steeped in wedding preparations and our house was full of relatives helping with the wedding meal?

From the misty windows I saw the words 'Gulf Air' written in Arabic and English on the doors of the airline's office and imagined myself one day buying a ticket to go to Hamid in Kuwait. It seemed that the fate of our generation is separation, from our country or our family. We are ready to go anywhere in search of the work we cannot find at home. Hamid says that there are many Sudanese in Kuwait and he hopes that in the next year or so the girls and I will join him. Every week I talk to him on the telephone, long leisurely conversations. We run up huge telephone bills but seem to be unable to ration our talking. He tells me amusing stories of the emirs whose horses he cures. In Sudan, cattle die from starvation or disease all the time, cattle which are the livelihood of many people. But one of the country's few veterinary surgeons is away, working with animals whose purpose is only to amuse. Why? So that his daughters can have a good education, so that he can keep up with the latest research in his field. So that he can justify the years of his life spent in education by earning the salary he deserves. And I thought of Taha's short life and wondered.

In Regent Street the conductor had to shake himself from his lethargy and prevent more people from boarding the bus. The progress of the bus was slow in contrast to the shoppers who swarmed around in the brightly-lit streets. Every shop window boasted an innovative display and there were new decorative lights in addition to the streetlights. Lights twined around the short trees on the pavements, on wires stretched across the street. Festive December lights. Blue, red, green lights, more elaborate than the strings of bulbs that we used in Khartoum to decorate the wedding house.

But the lights for Taha's wedding did not shine as they were meant to that night. By night-time he was already buried and we were mourning, not celebrating. Over the period of mourning, the wedding dinner was gradually eaten by visitors. The women indoors, sitting on mattresses spread on the floors, the men on wobbling metal chairs in a tent pitched in front of our house, the dust of the street under their feet. But they drank water and tea and not the sweet orange squash my mother and her friends had prepared by boiling small oranges with sugar. That went to a neighbour who was bold enough to enquire about it. Her children carried the sweet liquid from our house in large plastic bottles, their eyes bright, their lips moist with expectation.

When Taha died I felt raw and I remained transparent for a long time. Death had come so close to me that I was almost exhilarated; I could see clearly that not only life but the world is transient. But with time my heart hardened and I became immersed in the cares of day-to-day life. I had become detached from this vulnerable feeling and it is good to recapture it and grieve once again.

Taha's life; I was not there for a large part of it but I remember the time he got engaged and my own secret feelings of jealousy towards his fiancée. Muddled feelings of admiration and a desire to please. She was a university student and to my young eyes she seemed so articulate and self-assured. I remember visiting her room in the university hostels while Taha waited for us outside by the gate, hands in his pockets, making patterns in the dust with his feet. Her room was lively, in disarray with clothes and shoes scattered about and colourful posters on the wall. It was full of chatting roommates and friends who kept coming in and out to eat the last biscuits in the open packet on the desk, borrow the prayer mat or dab their eyes with kohl from a silver flask. They scrutinised my face for any likeness to Taha, laughed at jokes I could not understand, while I sat nervously at the edge of a bed smiling and unable to speak. Later with Taha we went to a concert in the football grounds where a group of students sang. I felt very moved by a song in the form of a letter written by a political prisoner to his mother. Taha's bride afterwards wrote the words out for me, humming the tune, looking radiant; and Taha remarked on how elegant her handwriting was.

In the shop windows dummies posed, aloof strangers in the frenzied life of Regent Street. Wools, rich silks and satin dresses. "Taha, shall I wear tonight the pink or the green?" I asked him on the morning of the wedding. "See, I look like... like a watermelon in this green." His room was an extension of the house where a verandah used to be, a window from the hall still looked into it, the door was made of shutters. He never slept in his room. In the early evening we all dragged our beds outdoors so that the sheets were cool when it was time to gaze up at the stars. If it rained Taha did not care, he covered his head with the sheet and continued to sleep. When the dust came thick, I would shake his shoulder to wake him up to go indoors and he would shout at me to leave him alone. In the morning his hair would be covered with dust, sand in his ears and his eyelashes. He would sneeze and blame me for not insisting, for failing to get him to move inside.

He smiled at me in my green dress, his suitcase, half-filled, laying on the floor. He leaned against the shutters, holding them shut with his weight. Through them filtered the hisses and smells of frying, the clinking of empty water glasses scented with incense and the thud of a hammer on a slab of ice, the angry splinters flying in the air, disintegrating, melting in surrender when they greeted the warm floor. Someone was calling him, an aunt cupped a hand round her mouth, tongue strong and dancing from side to side she trilled the ululation, the joy cry. When others joined her the sound rose in waves to fill the whole house. Was it a tape or was it someone singing that ridiculous song, "Our bridegroom like honey. Where can you ever find another like him?" To answer my question about the dress, he told me words I knew to be absurd but wanted to believe: "Tonight you will look more beautiful than the bride."

Heading north we passed Regent Park and the Central Mosque and all was peaceful and dark after the congestion of the shopping centre. I was glad that there were no more coloured lights for they are cheerful but false. I had held others like them before in my hands, wiping the dust off each bulb and saying to Taha, "How could you have taken them from the electrician when they were so dusty?" And he had helped me clean them with an orange cloth that he used for the car, because he was in a hurry to set them up all around the outside of the house. I had teased him, saying that the colours were not in an ordered pattern. We laughed together trying to make sense of their order but they were random, chaotic. Then Hamid, who was his friend, arrived and said he would help set them up. I asked Taha to get me a present from Nairobi where he was going for his honeymoon and Hamid had looked directly at me, laughed in his easy way and said without hiding his envy, "He is not going to have time to get you any presents." At that time, Hamid and I were not even engaged and I felt shy from his words and walked away from his gaze.

It was the lights that killed Taha. The haphazard, worn strings of lights, that had been hired out for years to house after wedding house. A bare live wire carelessly touched. A rushed drive to the hospital where I watched a stray cat twist and rub its thin body around the legs of our bridegroom's death bed. And in the crowded corridors, people squatted on the floor and the screams for Taha were absorbed by the dirty walls, the listless flies and the generous who had space and tears for a stranger they had never met before.

My mother, always a believing woman, wailed and wept but did not pour dirt on her head or tear her clothes like some ignorant women do. She just kept saying again and again, "I wish I never lived to see this day." Hamid maybe had the most shock for he was with Taha when he was setting up the lights. Later he told me that when they buried Taha he had stayed at the graveside after the other men had gone. He had prayed to strengthen his friend's soul at its crucial moment of questioning. The moment in the grave, in the interspace between death and eternity when the Angels ask the soul, "Who is your lord?" and there must be no wavering in the reply, no saying "I don't know." The answer must come swiftly, with confidence; and it was for this assurance, in the middle of what must have been Taha's fear, that Hamid prayed.

I had been in London for nearly seven months and I told no one about Taha. I felt that it would sound distasteful or like a bad joke, but electricity had killed others in Khartoum too, though I did not know them personally. A girl in my school was cleaning a fridge squatting barefooted in a puddle of melted ice with the electric socket too close. And a young boy once urinated at the foot of a lamp light which had a base from which wires stuck out, exposed. The girl's younger sister was in my class and the whole class, forty girls, went in the school bus to visit the family at home. On the way we sang songs as if we were on a school picnic and I cannot help but remember this day with pleasure.

With time, the relationship between my family and Taha's bride soured. Carefully prepared dishes ceased to pass between my mother and hers. In the two *Eids*, during which we celebrated in one the end of the fasting month of Ramadan and in the other the feast of sacrifice, our families no longer visited. Out of a sense of duty, my parents had proposed that she married another of my brothers but she and her family refused. Instead she married one of her cousins who was not very educated, not as much as Taha at any rate. Sometimes I would see her in the streets of Khartoum with her children and we would only greet each other if our eyes met.

In Taha's memory, my father built a small school in his home village on the Blue Nile. A single classroom built of mud to teach young children to read and write. The best charity for the dead is something continuous that

Illustration by Ruth Bailey

goes on yielding benefit over time. But like other schools it kept running into difficulties: no books, costly paper, poor attendance when children were sometimes kept at home to help their parents. Yet my father persevered and the school had become something of a hobby for him in his retirement. It is also a good excuse for him to travel frequently from the capital to the village and visit his old friends and family. What my mother did for Taha was more simple. She bought a *zeer* – a large clay pot – and had it fastened to a tree in front of our house. The *zeer* held water, and it was covered by a round piece of wood on which stood a tin mug for drinking. Early in the morning, I would fill it from the fridge and throughout the day passers, hot and thirsty from the glaring sun, could drink, resting in the shade of the tree. Here in London, I had come across the same idea in benches placed in gardens and parks where people could rest. My mother would never believe that anyone would voluntarily sit in the sun, but then she had never seen cold, dark evenings like these.

It was nearly time for me to get off as the bus had long passed Lords Cricket Ground, Swiss Cottage and Golders Green. My stop was near the end of the route and there were only a few passengers left. After dropping me off the bus will turn round to resume its cycle. And my grief for Taha comes in cycles as well, over the years, rising and receding away. Like the appearance of the West Indian conductor, it is transient and difficult to predict. Perhaps he will be on the bus tomorrow evening. "Like them Christmas lights?" he will ask, and, grateful to see a familiar face amidst the alien darkness and cold, I will say "yes, I admire the coloured lights."

Meg Bateman

Cìocharan

An glasadh an là
tha thu ag òl gu dian,
do shùilean ag amharc bhuat
gun bhrìgh nan duinne dhomh;
tha ùghdarras sa ghrèim
a tha aig do dhà làimh air a' chìch,
is d'òrdagan a' pronnadh mo bhronn
ri caismeachd dhiomhair.

Feasgar nì tu brìodal:
nì tu dinneadh air an t-sine,
is nì tu gàire 's i ag èirigh,
nì tu caogadh ri Dad mun cuairt oirre
is briosgaid na do dhòrn...

ach den oichdhe
cha chuilean meata thu –
cha tàlaich pòg air do bhilean thu
no duanag ga cagairt na do chluais –
spìonaidh do chorragan mo ghùn
agus le raoic asad dhan dorchadas
agraidh tu do chòir mar bu dual.

An Còigeamh Latha Deug den Fhaoilteach, 1991

Bha an seòmar ciùin geal mar eaglais
nuair a dhùisg mi an-diugh 's mo ghaol ùr rim thaobh,
a chuinnleinean a'lasadh an solas na maidne,
is tharraing mi a cheann rim uchd
air tuil thoileachais
cho buidhe 's cho fàsmhor ris a' chiad latha.

A-nochd spreadhaidh na bomaichean (san dol seachad)
beòil a dheoghail bainne bho chìch,
buill a dh'fhàs cruinn air bàrr na talmhainn,
's iad a'sracadh stuth na sìth' –
feòil ar carthannais,
a'slaodadh fiù's nan eun geala a-nuas dhan drabasdachd.

Nursling

In the grey of the dawn
you drink intently,
your eyes gaze ahead,
their brownness tells me nothing;
there is authority in the hold
of your two hands on the breast:
your toes knead my belly
to a rhythm of their own.

In the evenings you grow fond:
you press in the nipple
and laugh as it rises,
peeping round it at Dad
with a biscuit in your fist...

but at night
no tamed pup you –
no kiss on the lips can soothe you
or ditty whispered in your ear –
your fingers tear at my gown
as roaring at the darkness
you claim your hereditary right.

January 15th, 1991

The room was quiet and white like a church
when I woke today, my new love at my side,
his nostrils flaming in the morning light,
and I drew his head to my breast
on a flood of happiness
as golden and expansive as the first day.

Tonight (in the passing) bombs blast away
mouths that sucked milk from breast,
limbs that grew round on the crops of the earth,
ripping the stuff of peace –
the flesh of our humanity,
dragging even the white birds down in the obscenity.

A' Cur Bhruadairean Dhiom

Tha am feasgar ciùin,
an t-adhar san uinneig
gun smàl...
Isd, m' eudail,
na bruidhinn an dràsd,
tha taibhsean a'dol siar.

Chan e fear àraidh a chaoininn
ach beatha de mhiann,
gach roghainn neo-thaghte
gam threigsinn
air do shàileabh, fhir bhàin.

Dèan caithris leam
gus an tèid iad à sealladh.
Cha tig iad nar dàil, oir
is euchdaiche na iad
do shiol nam bhroinn, is dèine
bhios gul ar ciad-ghin
nuair a thogas tu e os àird.

Dha Mo Naoidhean
Air Dhuinn Tilleadh Bhon Ospadal

(le spèis do Chatrìona Montgomery)

Bha dùil a'm gum biodh tu agam
nad phasgan geal nam uchd
ri taobh na mara
fo na craobhan
san domhan àrsaidh ùr...

'S ann tha mi ga do shlaodadh
tro John Lewis, Mothercare is Boots
an tòir air bath dhut. Pampers,
pùdar Johnson, sling is pram;
an aon bhoile a-rithist an-dè:
changing-mat, cotton-wool a dhìth...
is an càr air chall oirnn
sa char-park multi-storey.

A Letting Go Of Dreams

The evening is calm,
the sky in the window
without stain...
Hush, my love,
don't talk now –
ghosts are going by.

No one man do I mourn
but a lifetime's longing,
every unmade choice
slipping from me
because of you, fair man.

Watch with me
till they are out of sight.
They will not hurt us, for
more potent than they
your seed in my womb, keener
the cry of our firstborn
when you raise it up on high.

To My Baby
On Our Return From Hospital

(with recognition of Catriona Montgomery)

I thought that I would have you,
a white bundle in my breast,
beside the sea
under the trees
in the ancient new world...

Insteard I am lugging you
round John Lewis, Mothercare and Boots,
looking for a bath for you, Pampers,
Johnson's Baby Powder, a sling and pram;
the same madness yesterday;
a changing-mat and cotton-wool...
and the car lost
in the multi-story car-park.

Ach san tìde seo de dh'aodannan
a' siubhal nan shopping malls
(fad' o shuaimhneas mara is coille)
aig check-out is ciudha
nochdaidh dhutsa
fàilte is
bàigh.

Mo naoidhean ùr,
dh'ionnsaich thu gliocas dhom,
mo naoidhean gaoil,
dh'ionnsaich thu dòchas dhomh
is tu toirt orm
m' earbs'
a chur sa linn san tug me beò thu.

Dealachadh

Uair 's a-rithist chanadh iad,
"Tha thu airidh air tuilleadh. Leig leis
a bheatha fhèin a chur an òrdugh…"
is iad a' sgrùdadh m'aodainn
mar gum b'e seòrsa de dh'amadan naomh mi.

Cha b'e naomhachd bu choireach
a leig mi seachad gach càineadh,
is cha b'e amaideas
a chùm an droch chàradh mi,
ach dòchas…

…Dòchas dhan leannan
a dhùisg annam a' chuid a b'fhèarr,
dha nach d'rinn mi sòradh mu aon nì…
dòchas dhan athair
dhan deàlraich sùilean a leanaibh…

Agus ge b'oil le fèin-mheas,
ge b-oil le misneachd,
cha b'iad sin a thug an dealachadh gu buil:
is ged nach robh dòigh eile ann,
cha b'e idir nach robh de ghaol ann.

But in this tide of faces
cruising the shopping malls
(far from peace of sea or wood)
at check-out and queue
you are shown
welcome and
tenderness.

My newborn child,
you've taught me patience,
my beloved child,
you've taught me hope,
as you force me
to trust in this age
in which I gave you life.

Published by the Six Towns Poetry Festival, 1995

Separation

Again and again they said:
"You deserve better. Let him
sort out his own life…"
and they'd scrutinise my face
as if I were some sort of holy fool.

It was not holiness
that made me ignore each rebuke,
nor was it foolishness
that held me in a wretched state;
it was hope…

…Hope for the sweetheart
who woke in me all that was best,
to whom I grudged nothing…
hope for the father
for whom his child's eyes shine…

And in spite of self-respect,
and in spite of courage,
those did not bring about the separation;
and though there was nothing else for it,
by no means was there no love.

Refugees

Deborah Moffatt

At breakfast, Dan studies the map, as he does every morning, choosing the route that they will take that day. "We'll take this green road up to Donegal," he suggests, running his finger along the map, "and then we'll turn off and go over to the coast. How's that?"

Rachel nods. That will be fine. Dan can choose any route, take her anywhere he likes. He can drive her to the end of the earth if he wants, and Donegal looks like it may well be the end of the earth. On the map, the north-west corner of Ireland appears desolate and bare. There are no big cities, few towns that Rachel can see, only a network of pale roads crisscrossing a vast expanse of beige countryside.

"Killybegs, Kilcar, Carrick, Glencolumbkille." Dan reads out the names of places they'll see. "There are two ancient ruins; one at Glencolumbkille, another just south of there." He turns the map over to read about the ruins. "Portal dolmens, souterrains, and cairns. Sounds good, huh?"

"Yeah." Rachel yawns. She's exhausted. This Bed and Breakfast existence is tiring. She's not used to rising so early. This is supposed to be a holiday, but it seems more like hard work, having to get up for breakfast, spending every day on the move, sleeping every night in a strange bed.

Dan notices her yawning. "Come on!" he says. "We'd better get moving, or you'll fall asleep."

Dan won't let Rachel rest. He thinks that would be the worst thing for her. He's afraid that if she stays too long in one place, stays quiet for any length of time, she'll start to think, start to brood, start to cry. He thinks it's important for her – for both of them – to keep active. So every day they keep busy, driving willy-nilly around Ireland, searching for ancient ruins and beautiful views and quaint villages. They are in and out of the car all day, jumping out to look at this and that, stopping here for a coffee, there for lunch; they keep going until it's almost too late to find a place to stay, and then there's always a panic, looking for a Bed and Breakfast with a vacancy. Once they've found a room for the night, they go out again to eat a hurried supper, and then they sip Guinness in a pub until closing time. Finally, they go to bed. Dan falls asleep as soon as his head hits the pillow, but Rachel usually tosses and turns half-way through the night. Now she's so tired she can hardly keep her eyes open. Dan pinches her arm, tells her to wake up. "Let's go," he says. "I can't wait to see Donegal."

It was Dan's idea to come to Ireland. He wanted to take Rachel on a holiday after the baby died. He thought it would be good for her – good for them both – to get away from home and work and all their worries and cares. He wanted to spend a few weeks in a foreign country, seeing new places, meeting new people, just having fun. He thought they could forget about the baby if they took a nice long holiday in Ireland.

But that isn't possible. Rachel can't forget the baby. It was horribly deformed. It had stumpy arms and legs sticking out at crazy angles from its twisted trunk. Its skin was shrivelled, rough, and a terrible colour, a sickly yellow, almost green. Its face was distorted, the eyes long and narrow, two grim little slits, and the mouth wide, gaping. The nose was flattened, almost non-existent; there was no chin at all. Rachel couldn't look at the baby. She couldn't bear to think that such a thing had once been part of her body. It shamed her; she didn't want anyone to see the baby, didn't want anyone to see her. All she wanted was to be left alone in her disgrace.

But she was not left alone. While the baby lived, Rachel was surrounded by social workers and hospital chaplains who promised her that raising the handicapped child would be the most rewarding experience of her life. When the baby died, medical researchers came to Rachel's bedside, carrying clipboards, shuffling papers and asking questions about her personal life. They wanted to know whether she'd drunk alcohol, or coffee, or tea, or even milk during her pregnancy. Did she smoke cigarettes, or marijuana, or use any illegal substances before the birth? Did she stay up late, or sleep lazily all day? Did she have sex with her husband – or with anyone else? – when she was pregnant? The researchers asked their questions briskly, bluntly, jotting down Rachel's answers without comment, and with every prying question they seemed to imply that there was some grave defect in Rachel's character, some terrible deformity of the soul which had infected and blighted and destroyed her poor innocent baby.

Now, Rachel doesn't dare look in the mirror; she's afraid she'll see that deformity exposed in her face, in the look in her eye. She can't bear to look at her body; she closes her eyes when she's dressing, and when she's in the bath or the shower she stares at the ceiling. What if she should glance down and find that her skin, like the baby's, is shrivelled and rough and yellow, or that her limbs are stumpy and malformed? She can't look Dan in the eye, and mercifully, he doesn't look at her. They spend the day looking at other things: at the map, at the ancient ruins, at the scenery.

They don't talk to each other, either, not really. They speak; Dan says something, and then Rachel says something, but nothing they say has any meaning or importance. They don't listen to each other. In the car, they listen to music; they play a tape of jolly Irish dance music, over and over again, never really paying much attention to it. In public places – in cafés and restaurants and most of all in pubs – they listen to the conversations of people around them; it seems as though the Irish never stop talking, and Rachel is grateful for that. At night, in a warm pub, she's happy to be in Ireland, listening to the lovely lilting sound of other people talking.

But by day, she thinks that Ireland isn't really the best place for her to be. As they drive through the villages on the way to Glencolumbkille, Rachel seems to see nothing but babies. Everywhere she looks, women are pushing prams, parading along the street with strings of toddlers following behind. The children are all very pale, and small, and thin, Rachel notices; they look anaemic, under-nourished. Many of them are crying.

Dan is talking about moving to Ireland, for good. "The pace of life is slower here," he says. "Everything is more relaxed, more natural." He slows the car and crawls through Carrick, beaming at the people in the street: the women with their screaming children, the old men with red faces and bandy legs. "At home, we rush around too much. It isn't healthy, the way we live there."

Rachel thinks she knows what he's trying to say. He's blaming the way they live, blaming the way *she* lives, blaming her for everything that's happened. "Well, it's no better here!" she says. "The men drink themselves into the grave and the women have babies until they drop. I don't call that healthy, or relaxed, or anything."

"Rachel! Don't be such a bigot!" Dan slaps his hand on the steering wheel. "There's more to the Irish than whisky and babies!"

"I'm not a bigot," Rachel protests. "I'm just practical. I couldn't live here, not for the rest of my life."

"Well, I could," Dan says. "And damn it, I can't go back to – to all that. After what's happened, I can't face going home, Rachel. I just can't!"

A dog runs in front of the car. Dan blares the horn and stamps on the brake. Rachel covers her face with her hands. She mustn't cry! Dan mustn't lose his temper! They sit in silence, breathing deeply, hiding their eyes from each other, refugees from their own lives. After a few minutes, Dan starts to drive again. He plays the tape of Irish music, turning the volume up loud so that they can't possibly talk.

At Glencolumbkille, he runs around the ruins, examining the dolmens, the souterrains, the cairns. Rachel sits on a stone, watching him. The site depresses her; it's really no more than a graveyard. The ruins are impressive, but lifeless, relics of a time long ago. It seems to Rachel that there is a smell of death in the brown swampy grass that surrounds the site.

"Come on," she says, near tears. "Let's go. I'm bored."

Dan follows her back to the car. "We'll skip the other site," he says. "It looks as if it's in the middle of a bog, anyway. We'll take a walk, how about? Get some fresh air into our lungs; that's what we need."

They head back towards Carrick. Dan asks Rachel to give him directions; he wants to take a road out towards Carrigan Head. "We'll see the cliffs of Slieve League from there," he explains. "The highest cliffs in Ireland. That should be something!" They take a few wrong turns; Rachel isn't very good at reading the map. She can tell Dan is getting irritated.

"This must be it," he says, doubtfully, when they come to a gate that blocks the road. "From here we walk."

They climb over the gate and start up the road. The hill is steep, but the road winds gently back and forth. After a while, Dan suggests that they make their own way up the grassy hill-side. Off the road, the ground is muddy, slippery, and the slope much steeper, but Rachel doesn't mind the climb. She doesn't think about it, just keeps on going, one foot after another, inching up the side of the hill. She feels that each step is carrying her farther from her misfortune; if only she could keep climbing forever!

When they reach the top of the hill, Dan looks out over the water. "Slieve League should be right over there," he says, but the mountain is hidden behind a thin mist of low-hanging clouds. "Just our luck!" Dan complains. He paces around in a tight circle, trying to catch his breath.

"Hey – look!" He drops to his knees, pokes his finger at the ground. "Look at this!"

"At what?" Rachel gasps. She's having trouble breathing, too. She's exhausted, but she doesn't dare say so to Dan. She knows that he can't bear her tiredness, her weakness. He wants her to be strong, resilient, in spite of everything.

"Frogs!" He points to a speck on the ground. "See? There's one. And another. There's millions of them, Rachel! Little baby frogs!"

Rachel sees them, a slithery, slimy mass of tiny frogs, hopping and jumping and sliding all over the mucky hill-side. She steps back, startled. They are everywhere, all around her, underfoot; one is climbing up her boot. "Ugh!" she cries, kicking her foot in the air, trying to get rid of the frog. "Oh, disgusting! Oh, Dan – they're horrible!" She starts to cry. "Come on!" she begs him. "Let's go back to the car!"

"For God's sake, they're just frogs!" he says. "Don't be an idiot!" He stamps over to her, shakes her. "What the hell is wrong with you?" he yells, allowing his anger to break out, at last, as Rachel gives in to her tears. "Silly fool! Afraid of frogs! Jesus Christ!" He turns away, bends down to study the frogs once more. After a minute or two he says, gently, "Come on, Rachel, look again. They're kind of cute, really. And there are so many of them! I can't get over it. God – what if every single one of these frogs was a prince?" Dan laughs at his little joke.

Rachel takes another look at the frogs. Maybe they aren't so horrible, after all. She reaches down, plucks one from the ground. It sits in the palm of her hand, blinking at her, and then dives back into the grass. "I guess that one wasn't a prince," she says, trying to make a joke of her own.

Dan doesn't laugh. "None of them are, Rachel," he says. "They're all just frogs; we both know that." He stands up, stuffs his hands in his pockets. "Do you want to go back now?"

"To the car?" Rachel looks over Dan's shoulder. The clouds have drifted out to sea, and the steep high cliffs of Slieve League are gleaming like a wall of ice in the sudden glare of the sun.

"I meant, do you want to go back home?" Dan explains.

"I don't know; it's not so bad here," Rachel says. "Look – you can see the mountain now."

Dan glances at the cliffs. "Yeah. Great." He turns back to Rachel, looks her in the eye. For the first time since the baby was born, she looks back at him. She doesn't see anger, or blame, or horror, or any of the terrible things she expected to see in his eyes; she sees only a reflection of her own bewildered grief. "Well?" he asks. "What do you want to do? Do you want to keep on going, or what?"

Beyond Slieve League, the Atlantic Ocean stretches out, cold and gray and bleak. They can't keep on going; from here, there is nowhere to go.

"I guess we'll have to go home sooner or later," Dan admits, taking Rachel's hand and leading her back down to the car.

Elise McKay

Washday blues

Steaming iron, spitting hiss;
once days had names
like Washing Day, and then
the Day to Iron.

Now rummaging through man-made fibres,
distressed jeans and drip-dry shirts,
I think of flat irons
propped on bricks before a glowing fire;
the smell of cotton, just too damp;
how creases could be smoothed away.

Not all delight, those washday blues,
when rain stopped play,
the boiler fire refused to draw,
the Acme didn't live up to its name.
But O the joy of flapping sheets,
white over green,
the smell of sun and breeze.
Exhausted pride.

Now sleek machines, steam at a touch
mean wrinkles don't arrive so soon.
But how to deal with man-made problems,
fibres of decay?
Somewhere behind our farthest thoughts
white sheets still blow;
but where's the iron now
will smooth a troubled world away?

Illustration by Ruth Bailey

Orcadia

1   The snow came, at first slowly,
     then suddenly, filling the dark
     with a flurry of snowflakes
     brushing the pane.
     And I can't fix on one flake
     to follow it home.

     Only memory traces its path
     down the glass; sees a ship
     plunging on through a mesmer of foam,
     and dazzled by seaspray,
     scattering spume, loses again
     the impossible 'one'.

     The wake widens out to break, far away,
     on a scatter of islands, too many to name –
     Eynhallow, Egislay, Wyre...

2   One land; an ocean of islands.
     History crushed into tombs
     or thrusting stones to the sky.
     The sea sounds from every noust.
     From every rock ripples spread.
     Sea and land locked together,
     linked by invisible strands.

     Though over each island
     the same wind calls,
     the same sun flickers
     on cormorants, seals;
     the freshness of seapinks,
     the wisdom of shells –

     yet they are not the same;
     one, but not one.

3   Here, there are layers,
     separate, but connecting.
     Stone circles interrupt the land.
     Farmers, ploughing, break through
     into history.
     In chambered tombs
     the sun lingers, momentarily,
     lighting up runes.
     An axe wound on a Viking skull.
     Layers upon layers.

Amongst them we wander,
unsure –
between then and now,
between sea and land.
Here there are no answers, only peace –
peace in a seabird's haunting call.

4 To fly back over the islands,
lying green upon misty blue,
is to see them pass so swiftly
they might well be one.

Back to the present,
and the snow still softly falling.
A single flake becomes a storm,
a drop of water, spray;
and, left behind, the islands
slip, connected, into memory.

To be complete is all.

Watcher on the hill

There is no silence.
Always something stirs;
wind in the grasses,
susurration of leaves.

From hill's top
the house lies low.
Windows stare blankly back.
A shadow flits across
the blind.

To be unseen is all.
Slip down behind larch trees,
greening for spring;
pines guarding dark.

Come nearer,
always nearer,
to where a door hangs
on uneasy hinge.

The old man stares
at nothing.
His eyes are blue, opaque.
What can they see?

He drops his lids.
Heavy shuttered eyes,
impossible to read,
leave revealed hands,
tight clenched,
white-knuckled;
aware.

The blind can sense
when they are not alone.

John Purser

Homage to Jack Yeats

The light, half indigo half white:
bog asphodel, delicate tormentil,
hinted in heather shadows

a glint of peat-stained water, and the glow
of pale bog-cotton tufts:
soon, a short cool breeze, and dawn.

The man, half-raised,
with gentle summons
extends an arm
crooked at the elbow, wrist curved, palm
cupped to receive and give
due homage:

the white horse
alert from its own wanderings
tosses a wilful head
acknowledging their bond
though his unwinking eyes
see other and beyond.

The man has slept no more
than needful, tall boots
still on.

          Who knows
what strange salvation
travels by horse and man
through ignorant lands,
their needs unthought of,
suffering unbought:
But they have fodder:

from those secret hours,
alone, cool, passionate,
comes an old knowing
that will hold their fancies
through the hot stumbling
of a dusty road,
whose fiery angels, book and vial
– all the prophetic threats –
will be of little consequence
to the white horse, the shadow man:

for they have seen before the dawn and,
in the long day-span
of the summer light,
know, now and for ever,
that there is no night.

Glen Scaladal

I trudge the ridge and furrow
of old lazy-beds: the loss and gain
where the cas-crom, heavy hilted,
long-footed, drained the land.
Now the land weeps, deserted,
choked with rain.

These written griefs
frowning and weeping
through the green-glowing glen
remain unspoken:
they are home for the iris,
stately and fine,
and burial ditch for the spent ewe,
her loins plundered by foxes –
the torn womb reveals
a small wet eyeless head.

There are no children here
whose supple hands
would have been asked to ease
that hard delivery:
and thinking of the lambs of all the world I hear
only the voice of a child running
mad-cap to her mother's woollen skirt
across sunlit Glen Scaladal,
and in that cry the perilous call
that searches still
for the warm comfort of humanity.

Amoretti XIV

We suffer the rose go wild
to straggle in a sky
of north wind
testing old desires.

It has nothing:
nothing to show for itself
but bare sticks –

and a hint of impudence
where hairy shoots
probe through the muddy lawn
to mock mowers.

It is enough: it tells
what each knew in the heart:
that there is more than hope
for this old, much loved
up-start.

Amoretti XV

It is late autumn and the sea
piles up along the coast:
my small boat, crowded with creels
dangling flaccid bait,
tumbles her hull to the gunwale
in fitful glints of sun
shouldered aside
by the dark shadows of waves.

Drifting her in, I see
I cannot land alone:
the strip we cleared
on the wild boulder shore
rumbles with dragged rocks: I prepare
heroics: I shall
jettison the creels and swim,
towing the boat in my teeth
rope between my teeth.

But here you come, unbidden,
down through the steep green bracken
edging brown, past the tarred shed,
straight out into the waves and,
breats-deep in the tide,
take my plunging prow
and guide us round
to face the sea for our return to shore
where I unload a small catch –
which you praise,
stretching the sunlight,
brightening the darker days.

For My Daughter In Black

Out of what shadow will she step
unrecognised?

When her feet scuff the scarfed timber stage
may they feel
cushions of wild thyme,
cool water from Drinan well:
may the salt sweat in her eyes
be from the nudge of a wave,
her black leotard
a sealskin.

May she know at that time
nothing of herself,
wholly other:

even so,
let her be as loved
for what she truly is
as what may be

that she may know
to whom
with whom
she has come home.

For My Son Who Would Wear Motley

Not parti-coloured
I suppose – though
in that well-chested
almost breast-plated
heart of yours

march armies
led by white and gold
standards.
But there's no currency
in that exchange,
though you might have it so.

Wear what is yours of old:
a truce, twice signed,
on two sides of one cloth
of gold shot through with white,
white shot with gold.

A River That Flows On

The Folk Revival and the Literary Tradition in Scotland

Alec Finlay

For any Scottish writer who wishes to reconcile individual expression with a wider sense of national consciousness, questions of national identity and voice are raised – questions MacDiarmid so successfully and consistently brought to the fore. In his essay 'Dialectics of 'Voice' and 'Place': Literature in Scots and English from 1700'[1], Roderick Watson draws attention to this search for national identity, and the important part played in this by the oral tradition in Scotland in which personal expression is adapted to a satirical, social or politicised purpose. Hamish Henderson championed this energising force. His whole creative career epitomises the tendency in Scottish letters to privilege *speaking* over *writing*.

For few Scottish poets in this century has the immediacy and empathy of performance – the act of 'speaking' or 'singing' – been so essential. In his first published work, the *Elegies for the Dead in Cyrenaiaca,* there is a tension between the 'speaking' voices – the voices of the poet-witness, the Gaelic bard and the swaddy – and the 'writing' voice of the art-poet. This tension was a prelude to the Folk Revival, in which 'writing' gives way to 'speaking', to song.

After the *Elegies*, and despite their success, Henderson published few poems of substance. It appeared as if the expectations of him as a gifted poet would not be realised. In the *Honor'd Shade* flyting at the end of the 1950s MacDiarmid implied that Henderson had indeed failed as a poet; and, writing in his own defence, Henderson described the attitude he now held towards his art: "The final shape of a new long poem I have been working on eludes me... In any case I have come to set greater store by my songs 'in the idiom of the people' than by other kinds of poetry that I have tried to write." Here, as an ally, he quotes Burns, and the implied parallel is a revealing one, as our national poet also, in his last years, set aside poetry in favour of song.

The tensions in the *Elegies* had already gone some way to indicating that the poetic forms and tenor of Cambridge – where in the mid-1930s he had come under the influence of Auden, Eliot, and the other great Modernists – were an uneasy vehicle for the ideas and emotions Henderson wished to express. Not only were they distant from the communal arts that he had grown up with and the nationalist issues which now concerned him, but, more importantly, 'art-poetry' itself was no longer the only, the most natural outlet, for his creative voice. This was the reason why he also rejected the obvious alternative to the influences he came under at Cambridge, the new Scots vanguard formed by the Lallans Makars or the Clyde Group, who followed MacDiarmid's example. These aesthetic

1. 1. *Scotland: A Concise Cultural History.* ed Paul H. Scott. Mainstream, Edinburgh 1993.

decisions, which followed from the Folk revival to the flytings, were a response to existing patterns of the Scottish creative voice.

In the Spring of 1950, travelling on the prize-money he received from the Somerset Maugham Award, he set off for Italy. His reason for returning there is described in a letter to MacDiarmid (see page 53). Henderson first heard of Gramsci from his comrades in the *Resistenza*, then in 1950 he met his close friend, the economist Piero Sraffa at Cambridge. Henderson was one of the very first people outside of Italy to recognise Gramsci's political and philosophical importance, and receiving the collected works as they were published in Italy, their influence was immediate. Gramsci makes a crucial though unacknowledged appearance in the phrases, "a literature of presentification" and "pluralism of superstructure" in 'Flower of Iron and Truth' (see page 58). His writings shaped Henderson's campaign to revive the Scottish traditional arts over the course of the following decade.

An overtly political project, Henderson's journey to Italy was a turning aside from his literary career. The Folk Revival was consciously modelled on MacDiarmid's renaissance movement of the 1930s and 40s; however, its beginnings can still best be traced to a chance encounter, signalled in a letter Henderson received from his friend Ewan MacColl (see page 53). With Alan Lomax's arrival all of the elements that would gel into the modern Folk Revival had fallen into place.

The First years of The Folk Revival

Hamish Henderson was a born collector. It was a natural birthright of the oral culture to which he belonged. All through the war he had filled his notebooks with his own poems, songs and translations, and the songs, stories and bawdy verses of British, German and Italian soldiers. While still working on the *Elegies* in 1946, staying in the Lochboisdale hotel, he met Seamus Ennis and Calum MacLean. They were collecting in Scotland under the auspices of the Irish Folklore Commission, there being no equivalent Scottish institution. Calum later became the first full-time appointee to the School of Scottish Studies, and remained a friend and staunch ally of Henderson's until his tragically early death in 1960.

McCarthyism had forced Alan Lomax temporarily to quit America. He brought with him a tape-recorder; a new weapon in the armoury of the Revival. This made possible a fidelity to the oral tradition, a 'presentification' of the spoken and sung voice, allowing the oral arts to remain predominant, rather than print, which had always come to dominate in the past. Henderson summarised these influences:

> Gramsci's insights, combined with the experience I had gained during field-work with Alan Lomax and his tape-recorder, suggested one urgent need: that of placing examples of authentic native singing-styles, and – wherever possible – actual performances of good traditional artists within the reach of the young apprentice singers of the Revival...[2]

2. 'It Was in You That it A' Began: Some Notes on the Folk conference': Hamish Henderson in *The Peoples Past,* ed Edward J. Cowan, Polygon 1980

After the success of the first trip apprenticed to Lomax, the newly formed School of Scottish Studies financed a number of further collecting trips, and it was on these that Henderson first met Willie Mathieson, John MacDonald, John Strachan, all important 'source' singers, and then in 1953, Jeannie Robertson. The importance of this meeting was immediately clear. The short walk between the University Library in Kings College, Old Aberdeen, where he would study Gavin Greig's great folk-song collection, to Jeannie's house in nearby Causewayend, where he would often enough walk into an impromptu ceilidh or story-telling session, became symbolic of the gulf between academicism and the living tradition. It was this 'cultural apartheid' that he set about to remove once and for all.

In 1954 he was appointed a full-time research fellow at the School, and in the Summer of 1955 he returned on a collecting trip to his home town, Blairgowrie, where, as Maurice Fleming had informed him, there was a wealth of traditional material to be harvested amongst the workers who assembled at Berrytime. He was overwhelmed by the song, story and lore which flowed from the travelling people gathered for the berry-picking. Never had it been so clear to him that this was not a question of isolated survivors preserving old fragments of balladry. This was an alternative culture shared by the whole gathering, old and young:..[3]

This alternative culture was to become his new spiritual home. From the moment that he committed himself to the Folk Revival Henderson moved gradually closer to his childhood home; away from the Glasgow of John Maclean and the urban proletarian sympathies of the Clyde Group, back towards the North East, the land and its songs; and although Henderson never reneged on his political allegiance to Marxism and working-class culture, he now moved away from an urban poetry of commitment – another accusation of MacDiarmid's. Under the influence of Gramsci this commitment took on a new form. Devoting his creative energies to the world of farm workers and, more remote yet in social terms, that of the travellers, he found himself moving away from limited contemporary political and literary perspectives. His interest in the songs of the rural labouring classes was a far cry from the "lanely wishan wells" of pastoral sentimentality that he had criticised so strongly in the past, and he grasped the possibility of challenging the cultural hegemony that shaped the national voice, just as MacDiarmid had in the 1920s. The great difference in the political characteristics of their aesthetic was that, under the influence of Gramsci, Henderson felt able to remain true to his rural origins, whereas MacDiarmid was apparently persuaded that the urban proletariat was the only legitimate vehicle for progress. The reconciliation Henderson achieved is echoed in his 'John Maclean March', in which Neil, the Highland teuchter joins hands with Jock and Jimmy, and the red and the green are worn side by side.

3. Maurice Fleming, *Tocher 43,* School of Scottish Studies, Edinburgh University, 1991.

The relationship between the folk and literary traditions

In his critical writings Henderson has often returned to consider the curious and complicated interwoven relationship between the literary and oral traditions, which have been such a strong influence on his own creative voice, and the tendency amongst many of Scotland's greatest authors to carry this interplay to a natural conclusion, by setting aside authorial identity in favour of the communal identity of the folk tradition – Burns's songs being the most famous example. A kind of bastard child of this tendency is the frequency of the alias in modern Scottish literature, and MacDiarmid is, as Henderson says in his essay 'Alias MacAlias', the most fascinating example of this.

The desire for anonymity – or the communality which would eventually lead there – is at the root of Henderson's commitment to the Folk Revival. This explains his reluctance to publish his own songs, preferring to see them transmitted and gradually altered within the carrying stream, and it is the reason for his attempts to replace a literary model of authorship with one drawn from the very different models of the Folk tradition. The Revival emphasised interpretation over authorship, challenging conventional literary models. Henderson emphasizes the communality of folk compositions. This communal vision of the figure of the author contributed to the break with MacDiarmid, because, despite the challenging inconsistencies in MacDiarmid's own creative methods, the elder poet held resolutely to the sovereign power of the creative consciousness, embodied in the supreme achievements of the poet. In the controversy over MacDiarmid's use of unattributed quotations, most famously 'Perfect', Henderson's defence stressed the influence of the Folk tradition on MacDiarmid: "This acquisitive attitude to material from all sorts of sources is strongly reminiscent of the folk poet, who frequently appropriates lines or even whole stanzas from other poems or songs..." – here tradition and the *avant garde* tread toes.

However, it is equally true that the communal arts have their own problematical characteristics, most obviously a tendency to self-censorship. Henderson's idealistic commitment can be seen as an avoidance of a kind, born perhaps of his inability to commit his emotional self in the absolute personal sense that the greatest poetry demands: here again we return to his hesitancy as an author. The different choices he and MacDiarmid made were the truest responses to the nature of their own creative and emotional expression, as well as being a response to national and political ideals and precedents; and, in this sense, not only their battles but their creative personas fall into established patterns in Scottish culture.

In the latter part of the 1950s, as they manoeuvred for position, Henderson and MacDiarmid returned to their different interpretations of Burns's legacy. Burns was a crucial precedent for Henderson, as the most important creative influence on the first of the Modern Folk-song Revivals: "Burns set up a folksong-workshop of his own, and transformed, without seeming effort, our whole conception of the meaning of traditional art for society..."[4]

MacDiarmid's criticisms of the Burns cult are well known: but of particular relevance here is an essay that he published in 1952, 'Robert Fergusson: Direct poetry and the Scottish Genius' (published in the very same year that he made his speech of praise at the People's Festival ceilidh). This precedes the *Honor'd Shade* flyting by some seven years and is primarily an attack – his first public attack – on the fledgling Folk-song Revival. Fergusson represents the possibilities of a direct use of Scots speech as a literary language, allied to a firm political resolve, resistant to "all anglification"; a commitment to the poetry of city life and the urban proletariat; while Burns, at his worst, represents Scottish sentimentality, anti-intellectualism, political wavering, and implicitly a romanticised attachment to the rural poor. MacDiarmid's attacks on the Folk Revival come directly out of this political analysis. He castigates the 'dangerous' popularity of Folk-song, which encourages 'maudlin sentiment' and 'permanent juvenility', and is opposed to 'modern development', 'scientific progress', betraying the intellectual concerns of his own poetry. In his analysis folk-song is intricately connected with the social and historical conditions of the Scottish peasantry and rural labourers of the eighteenth and nineteenth centuries. In a letter towards the end of the *Honor'd Shade* flyting, he wrote that: "Mr Henderson evidently wants to stabilise people at a low level corresponding to a state of society that has virtually ceased to exist..." (19/1/60); and, in *Aesthetics in Scotland*, "the folk-song movement is hopelessly bogged down in senseless repetition and a hopelessly sentimental attitude to an irrecoverable past."

Need the oral tradition be any more tied to particular social and historical conditions than literature, than the renaissance MacDiarmid had forged? For MacDiarmid there is an ongoing argument between the two arbiters of the Scottish voice, 'writing' and 'speaking': *poetry*, which had up until now been the defining medium for the new cultural movement, and now *folk-song*, which for MacDiarmid was incapable of forming an *avant garde*, either culturally or politically, its popularity an inevitable compromise. For Henderson these forces were not competing but complimentary, and the achievement of any *avant garde* in Scotland was dependent on its respecting the integral balance in Scottish culture between literature and the Folk voice. One of the Revival's main aims was to graft the best of the traditional arts onto the urban population, reintegrating the culture of the rural regions with that of the proletariat – Comrie with Govan – reconciling the antagonisms MacDiarmid's political analysis perpetuated.

In letters to the Scottish press in 1948 Henderson defended the Renaissance, not on the grounds of the inherent 'Scottishness' of their work, but because they represented an *avant garde*. The Revival itself did

---

4. Hamish Henderson, sleeve-notes to *The Muckle Sangs,* Scottish Tradition, Tangent (TNGM 119/D)

42

not eschew the use of experiment and new technology: the crucial
influence of the tape-recorder has already been mentioned, and there are
also the examples of Ewan MacColl's famous series of radio ballads and
Timothy Neat's film and television documentaries. Although MacDiarmid
pointedly avoided acknowledging the parallels between the synthetic
manipulation of tradition he engineered some three decades before, and
the methods of the Folk Revival, Henderson saw that the folk idiom was
a source from which many of the Modernists had drawn.

Henderson and MacDiarmid share remarkably similar overall cultural
strategies: both dedicated to the reassertion of Scottish traditions, both
focusing on the relationship between voice, psychology and national
consciousness, both breaking what George Davie calls the 'crust of
custom'. MacDiarmid studied the literary Revivals of Norway, Catalonia,
and Ireland, and, following their example, he revived a modern literature
based on "the literary achievements of the classic periods in their own
country's past, when the language…had been in full flower."[5] Henderson
likewise set out to reconstruct Scotland's post-war vision of the folk
tradition – then as moribund and stereotyped as poetry had been in the
1920s – bringing the new source-singers to the fore, creating a new canon
based on the flower of traditional song.

In their flytings Henderson avoids attacking the poetry of MacDiarmid,
rather he concentrates on the political and social ideas which orbit around
his work. This reticence is explained by the particular importance
MacDiarmid's poetry held with respect to the Folk Revival. While
Henderson could happily cite the achievements of his poet, song-
composing and folk-song collecting predecessors, Burns, Scott and Hogg,
as evidence of the interwoven relationship between art poetry and the
folk tradition, he could not present a figure of equivalent literary stature
in the modern Revival. His insistence that MacDiarmid's poetry belongs
within this tradition is an attempt to do just this; and when he praises
MacDiarmid as "the greatest poet since Burns, who has devoted his life
to the cultural resurgence of his country", someone whose work
"exemplifies many of the best features of the marriage between folk-song
and art poetry…"[6], he is tying MacDiarmid to this role, as the comparison
with Burns confirms.

Henderson's later criticisms of MacDiarmid centre on what was really
an issue of 'faith': knowing that MacDiarmid was the only poet capable of
sustaining the new popular project in terms of art-poetry, he could not
forgive him for abandoning this possibility, and retreating into an
increasing distrust of anything tinged with populism. He retained his love
for art poetry, and in his commitment to a genuinely popular movement,
he valued held up MacDiarmid's great works of the period 1925–35,
especially 'The Seamless Garment', as supreme achievements. These
poems fused together intellectual ideas and the speech of the common

5. *The Crisis of the Democratic Intellect*, George Davie, Polygon, Edinburgh, 1986 pp104–5
6. Letter from HH to the *Times Educational Supplement*, 1975

Hamish Henderson & Sandy, Meadows, May 1990.　　　Photo: *Ian MacKenzie*

people. However, the success of the Revival only seemed to confirm MacDiarmid in his view that great art must, of necessity, be unpopular. Great poetry served 'the engagement between man and being', and this could never be expressed adequately in folk-song, rooted as it was in the physical world of the soil and the senses.

The Folk Revival was a synthetic means to reassert a traditional process. Henderson believed that once it was initiated, and modulated by the 'natural' influence of the living tradition, the movement would become self-perpetuating, as indeed it did. The songs and stories that he and others collected, particularly the examples discovered in the isolated world of the travellers, were tangible evidence that the 'ghostly voice', as Yeats called it, was still alive, still renewing itself in the carrying stream. The primary aim of the Revival was firstly to record these songs and stories, and secondly, and in a way even more importantly, to create a renewal of these traditions, especially amongst the young, so that this material could be preserved in its only true form, in living interpretation.

Despite MacDiarmid's disapproval, the Revival's heterogeneous mixture of traditional ballads and contemporary protest songs, skiffle and Music Hall, Dylan and MacBeath, was a creative stimulus every bit as rich as the heady mixture of Jamieson's Dictionary and racy Scots speech that had captured his imagination thirty years before. The Revival was a popular movement, and a democratic one, but it would be wrong to think that it did not present a certain hierarchy of artistic achievement. From the outset Henderson gave priority to the 'muckle sangs'; in this lay Jeannie Robertson's seminal importance and influence. His veneration of her interpretations asserts a 'classic' standard for the whole Revival movement – women are noticeably to the fore in the revival, as much as they are noticeably absent in the Renaissance, and this has many precedents, most famously Mary MacPherson ('Big Mary of the Songs') and Mrs Brown of Falkland. Jeannie Robertson's ballad interpretations were models of the traditional singer's art, as they were also a living connection with the voices of the past.

Henderson's contribution to the issue of voice follows on from and extends the cultural project MacDiarmid had begun in the 1920s. As MacDiarmid's ideas about the Scottish voice evolved, he journeyed backwards through time, from the vernacular Scots of his Langholm childhood, the Border Ballads, and the poetry of Ramsay, Fergusson and Burns, to the more ancient forms of Scotland's languages, to the Makars and the Gaelic tradition, and finally, though his readings in linguistics and anthropology, to the Celtic and pre-Celtic roots traced in his own idiosyncratic manner in *In Memoriam James Joyce*.

The *Golden Treasury of Scottish Poetry* which MacDiarmid edited while living on Whalsay was a high-point in the development of these ideas. This anthology was the primary statement Henderson encountered in the immediate post-war years. It includes many examples of folk-song. In his Introduction MacDiarmid argues in favour of a radical and more broadly-based understanding of the Scottish voice: Scotland's Latin and Gaelic poets, and the anonymous Ballads, are laid alongside the greatest works of the Makars and the modern Renaissance, in an alliance which is to form a bulwark against the insidious influence of anglification.

Although he rejected MacDiarmid's anglophobia, Henderson does take up this concern with linguistic diversity, and the Revival (including the example of his own songs), broadened this exploration of the old tongues. The primary difference between them is that MacDiarmid imagined a campaign whose eventual conclusion would be the renewal of Gaelic as the dominant national language – an argument paralleled by some of his most controversial comments about the 'true racial life' – while Henderson committed himself to an ongoing diversity, precisely because this was the best guarantee against such overbearing nationalist sentiments, as well as being a necessary challenge to the ascendancy of any single tongue – something Scotland has never had.

In his early critical writings, Henderson concentrated on the contemporary political and cultural dimensions of the voice issue, downplaying the historical dimensions and expressing his distrust of the 'literary-historical cross-talk' so beloved of poet-scholars, whose arguments he portrays as bourgeois mystification. In an article written in the same year as 'Flower of Iron and Truth', titled 'Lallans and all That'[7], 'presentification' is defined in a straightforward assertion: "the speech of the people is still a helluva lot nearer to the language of Burns than to the stringy argot of a BBC announcer", proof in itself that a 'contemporary and popular literature' could be achieved in the Scottish tongue. The limited scope of reference of these early articles is their greatest weakness; however, the origins of his own popular project can still be discerned in them, particularly in his insistent focus on the spoken voice. As Gramsci illuminates his political thinking, he extends his criticism towards the new aim of reuniting "Govan or Hamilton ... with Comrie or Lochboisdale"; but not with the intention of creating a single homogenous nation, a 'pluralism of superstructure', but rather he echoes the philosopher's vision of folk culture subverting the conventions of nationalism:

> [what] distinguishes folksong in the framework of a nation and its culture is neither the artistic fact not the historic origin; it is a separate and distinct way of perceiving life and the world, as opposed to that of official society[8]

A great song carries the emotional force of its performance; but also, resonating beneath this in the shimmering colours of a great singer's voice, is the imprint of an ancient artistic lineage, a communal timbre and historical richness, all of which reaches a peak in the art of the travellers. By the end of the first decade of the Revival Henderson was, just as MacDiarmid had before him, journeying through history and the deep subconscious undercurrents of the Scottish voice. The psychology, the

---

7. 'Lallans and All That', Hamish Henderson in *Conflict*, ed Norman Buchan, Glasgow University Socialist Club, March 1949.
8. Antonio Gramsci, from *Letteratura e Vita Nazionale*, Quoted by Duncan Glen in 'Poetry Becomes People' , Inter Arts, vol 1 no 7, October 1988)

pitch of emotional intensity embedded in the words and rhythms of an ancient song, is once again *alive*. It is a transcendent quality which vaults over the socio-historical barrier MacDiarmid erected around folk culture during the flytings.

Folk-song has consistently been identified with a golden age in Scottish culture. It reaches back beyond the debilitating linguistic dichotomy imposed in the seventeenth and eighteenth centuries, which forced Literate Scots "to carry two languages in their heads – English for writing, Scots for speaking; English for 'proper' occasions, Scots for real life", creating the "peculiarly Scottish dissociation of sensibility whereby, as Edwin Muir put it, Scotsmen felt in Scots and thought in English..."[9] Bitterly opposed to the psychological stunting and political compromise that Muir's analysis implied, MacDiarmid attempted to confront this history head-on. Common to these literary-based analyses is the impression that the great folk-songs are a voice from beyond this cultural catastrophe, untainted by the calamity from which our culture and national consciousness is still reeling. However, the picture Henderson paints contradicts this: the success of the Folk Revival, whose life-blood is fusion, proves the ongoing interaction between 'speaking' and 'writing', and his own work embodies and celebrates this part-literate, part-oral culture, which he was born to. As long as the folk idiom remains the most genuine outlet for an artist's emotion, it will endure.

Henderson's ideas on the question of voice – which were not drawn together until a retrospective essay, published in 1983, 'At the Foot o' yon Excellin' Brae' – extend this counter-argument. The essay favourably compares the Folk-song tradition with Scots art-poetry, and seeks to break open the bastion of MacDiarmid's cultural separatism: "a curious 'bilingualism in one language' has always been a characteristic of Scots folk-song at least since the beginning of the seventeenth century."[10] The criticism of Lallans becomes direct. It is described as a "self-conscious literary Scots" which "came increasingly to seem documentations of a sad case of arrested development." The underlying political currents rise to the surface, in a passage which repudiates MacDiarmid's absolutism: "The anonymous ballad-makers... were operating in a zone which ignored national and political boundaries." Then, making close reference to the distinctive qualities of the oral tradition, Henderson reasserts the uniqueness of the Scottish voice within a new internationalist perspective. "The unchallenged excellence of our ballad versions" is an achievement residing in:

> the actual nature of the language in which they are couched – in what we may term 'ballad-Scots'. This, the idiom in which the virtuoso song-makers were operating, is a flexible formulaic language which grazes ballad-English

9. *The Ballad and the Folk*, David Buchan, Routledge, Kegan & Paul, London 1972.
10. 'At the Foot o' Yon Excellin Brae: The Language of Scots Folk-Song', HH in *Scotland and the Lowland Tongue*, ed J. Derrick McClure, Aberdeen University Press, 1983; reprinted in *Alias MacAlias: Writings on Songs, Folk and Literature*, Hamish Henderson, Polygon, Edinburgh 1992.

along the whole of its length, and yet remains clearly identifiable as a distinct folk-literary lingo... [Thus] in the folk field as well as in the less agile literary Lallans, Scots may be said to include English and go beyond it.

This is a bold claim, one which consciously echoes MacDiarmid. He asserts the importance of the folk tradition, and redoubles the claim for the Scottish voice, or voices, which are no longer to be defined by the standardised conventions established by print, but rather in the plethora of spoken and sung voices of the Scottish people, and, in particular, in the interpretative styles of the great Revival singers.

Poets and Folkies

The Folk Revival was a natural forerunner of the new poetries that have flourished since the 1960s, which share the demotic vitality of folk-song. In his later years MacDiarmid held some famously controversial views. His uncanny ability to jumble together folk-song, the skiffle and beat movements, Concrete Poetry, the writings of Alexander Trocchi, and place them all on the same list of proscribed items, helped to solidify an alliance between folkies and poets. One of the most amusing episodes in the skirmishes between this younger generation and the Renaissance 'establishment' was the use of MacGonagall as a satirical club to whap over MacDiarmid's head, a weapon drawn straight from Henderson's arsenal.

Edwin Morgan and Henderson both wrote important essays which refer to the MacGonagall phenomenon, 'The Beatnik in the Kailyard'[11], and 'MacGonagall the What'[12]. Henderson's article, a comparison of the two Macs was calculated to infuriate MacDiarmid. It was a last riposte to the 1964 flyting, and a typically virtuoso display of knowledge of the folk tradition. In Morgan's case, the modernity that has always been a mark of his poetry seems at first to be at odds with folk culture; however, the similarity between his argument and Henderson's is telling. He takes up the argument against a divisive polarisation between Scots and English:

...it is a real and unavoidable incubus... [which] makes it all the more difficult for Scottish writers to develop integrally... when an exclusive choice is made... there may be some psychological loss... one that brings the constant hazard of a narrowing of outlook since Scottish speech itself is still very fluid in the range from broad Scots to standard English.'

Morgan's remarks about the benefits of "an unanguished flexibility in this matter of language" correspond with Henderson's heterogeneous sense of national voice.

These essays were part of a reaction against the paternalistic influence of the Renaissance. Morgan expressed the problem succinctly: "The Renaissance has begun to loosen its hold on life. It has allowed life both in Scotland and elsewhere, to move on rapidly and ceaselessly in directions it chooses not to penetrate." These were struggles for a new

---

11. *New Saltire Review*, no. 3, Edinburgh 1962
12. *Chapbook*, edited by Arthur Argo, Aberdeen 1965, reprinted in *Alias MacAlias*.

48

openness in emotional and political terms, but they were also a search for a more light-hearted and playful art. In Morgan's words, MacGonagall represents "some deep-rooted human feelings... some need of the Scottish soul..." This plea for a more honest appraisal of the Scottish character, including the sentimental and the fey, accompanied criticism of MacDiarmid, whose later work was described as suffering from "a lack of warmth, a failure or a banishing of ordinary human sympathy." Henderson echoed this in the strongest attack he was to make on MacDiarmid, in the 1964 'Folk-song Flyting':

> There are unresolved contradictions in Mr. MacDiarmid's whole approach to the problems of language and the folk arts... [He] has come to despise and reject the "people of his country's past" with all the ardour of a 17th century "saint" outlawing the folk-singing and dancing damned to outer darkness... [he is] the apostle of a kind of spiritual apartheid.

Looking again at the development of the Scottish voice, it is possible to see these fruitful interchanges between the folk and literary traditions; for instance, if we trace a line of development threading its way through the work of MacDiarmid and the 'Clyde Group', then through the Folk Revival, and the emergence of new urban folk-singers such as Matt McGinn and Adam McNaughtan, and 'Ding Dong Dollar' anti-Polaris songs, to the new poets of the 1960s, such as Ian Hamilton Finlay, whose *Glasgow beasts* is one of the clearest examples of the influence of the Folk Revival, and then later Tom Leonard, and extending into the present day with the work of John Byrne or W.N. Herbert and beyond.

This prolix Scottish voice has developed into an increasingly subtle expression of an individual, as well as a national psychology; a stasis within the constant interplay between the evolving spoken voice and the language of print, and an assertion of Scottishness that allows for diversity. If we are to draw any conclusions about this ongoing relationship between the folk and literary traditions, it will not be by holding fast to the antipathies between MacDiarmid and Henderson, to the positions they represented thirty or forty years ago. Henderson himself would be the first to agree that the Revival he fought for and defended now belongs within the period of 'MacDiarmidism' (as Angus Calder has named it), and the fact that he had at one time to oppose the man within that 'ism' simply bears out the different places they then occupied on the winding gyres of the communal and individual voices of Scotland.

Note: This essay is a shortened version of the Editor's Afterword which will appear in *The Armstrong Nose: Selected Letters of Hamish Henderson*, Polygon, Edinburgh, 1995. I would like to thank Alan Riach, Roderick Watson, Duncan Glen and Hamish Henderson for their comradely support – Alec Finlay, August 1995

Selected Letters

Hamish Henderson

To John Lehmann, 13 November 1944

Dear John Lehmann

These hills are a great breeding ground of blasphemy. The Partisans swear by Madonna the pig and Jesus the assassin, and in spite of Monty's old Orders of the Day his veterans in the Apennines are now much given to taking in vain the name of the God of Battles. Sitting round a fire in this mountain croft, the members of the 36th Garibaldi Brigade (Biaconcini) discuss the best ways of executing Fascists.

I'm getting into the habit myself. This morning our local river was in spate, and no jeeps could get across – no one has had the nerve to build a bridge yet as the area concerned is under immediate enemy observation – who should come along but an RC padre in his jeep, and start raising hell about nobody being allowed to cross. You'll never make it, Sir, says the CMP. The padre insists. The CMP holds his ground… I comment (*sotto voce*): If he wants to cross this bloody wadi he'll have to get out and walk on the waves!

I notice by my notebook that I promised you a letter about Florence, but I'm so *smemorizzato* and generally cack-brained now I can't recollect if I did write it or not. When I can concentrate I'm writing a poem about Alexandria now [third *Elegy*, 'Leaving the City'], which I'll let you have when it's finished. Luigi has written and dedicated to me a poem called 'Linea Gotica'. It's in alcaics!

From G.S. Fraser I got a letter which gives me quite a nostalgia for Cairo. He describes John Gawsworth who sounds an agreeable humbug, and has seen that soft-tongued satirical man John Spiers at a party … Christ, I'm in limbo now, marooned on the mountains of the moon. I'll not read 'A Walk in the Sun' yet – the irony is too devilish.

Yours, H. Henderson

PS: It's snowing again.

To Maurice Lindsay, 27 April 1946

Dear Maurice Lindsay

I've just received your letter of 4 April, which was forwarded on to me from Portree. A lot of things are much clearer to me now than before. The first is why I never got your first letter, and likewise why this second letter was not given to me by the nice little bit of stuff in Portree Post Office when I called in there ten days ago.

I'll give you five guesses. Or would you prefer fifty? – The reason is that by a readily understandable piece of verbal association you have transformed the name Hamish Henderson into Hamish Hamilton – the latter being as you know a well-known publisher. So that's the reason why Mairi in Portree told me there was no letter for Henderson – "but just the one for a Mr. Hamilton".

The only solution, I suppose, is to call myself in print what the North calls me – Seumas mac Eanruig. It's not so alliterative, but on the other hand is the real MacKay, as one might say. On the other hand, again, it would floor my Italian public. So what have you? I'll probably fall back on my Army Personal Number eventually!

Am glad to hear that the Govoni poem is to appear in *PS* 3: I had gathered it probably would from MacLellan[1]. As for the other two, you can certainly have 'Karnak' for *PS* 4, but I'm afraid 'Acroma' is no longer on the market.[2] Still I shall send you some more shortly if you would like to see them.

Poetry Scotland is a great thing, and I'm sorry that owing to my isolation among Panzerschrecks and Partisans I remained unaware of its existence for so long. However as MacL. may have told you I showed a copy of *PS* to some of our more interesting prisoners, including some Wehrmacht I.O.s and SS high-ups – some were quite cultured individuals – and they all without exception picked on Somhairle mac Gill Ean's poem as the most interesting thing in it. One asked – how typically Deutch this is! – for a Gaelic primer: he wanted to tackle this question of Scottish culture *vor allen Dingen grundsätzlich*. This in spite of the fact he was going to be shot and knew it.

There is also a great interest for Scotland in Italy: one of my Milanese friends, Luigi Castigliano, has already a good grasp of the vernacular – he writes in a letter: "There are 29,999 different words in *Ulysses*, and that should be muckle eneuch for a poor Eyetye; and now a flavouring with MacDiarmid!" – in two months with the 8/Argyll he learnt all there is to know about the clan Campbell and Inverary, and developed an addiction for pipe-music.

Another has sent me a *Cartolina dall' Italia* which you might like to have. It might look quite effective, being short, if printed in original and translation.

All the best,
Yours,
Hamish Henderson

TO THE *GLASGOW HERALD*, C. 1947 (NOT USED; COPY SENT TO C. M. GRIEVE)

Sir – The heavy-handed sarcasm of your Editorial Diarist at the expense of writers who experiment with Scots deserves an answer, despite its cheapness. For it is clear that the Diarist is unfamiliar with all the more important facts about the making of a poem, and about the nature of language. He is unaware, for example, that the linguistic problems which he parodies have existed for a good proportion of writers in every country, and in every age.

Take, for example, the famous eighteenth-century Italian poet Alfieri. He was a Piedmontese aristocrat who was brought up to speak a local dialect

---

1. Corrado Govoni, Italian poet: Henderson's translation of his 'Dialogue of the Angel and the Dead Boy' appeared in *Poetry Scotland* 3.
2. 'Karknak' and 'Acroma' are the eighth and sixth *Elegies* respectively.

(basically Italian, with a strong French flavouring), and also French, which was the language of the Turin court and particularly dominant in the Little Kingdom, just as English is here today. His acquaintance with Tuscan, the traditional Italian literary dialect (in which he afterwards wrote excellent verse), was in his youth almost nil. He relates in his autobiography with engaging candour that until he was well into his twenties he displayed no inclination to write, and very little to read, so that until manhood the incomparable treasure of Italian poetry was literally a closed book to him.

It was no accident that Alfieri's return from linguistic exile to the language of his country coincided with a revulsion towards all things French, which expressed itself both politically and personally. Indeed, this Gallophobia became towards the end of his life something of an obsession, for he declares in his *Vita* that the ugliest women he had ever seen were to be found in Paris!

However, the essential thing for lovers of literature (as against types with the mentality of your Editorial Diarist) is that he won through and wrote memorable verse from which his upbringing had almost totally estranged him.

In spite of the sneers of linguistic Quislings, who find it convenient to side with the big battalions of London press lords and Glasgow Englishmen, Scottish poets will find more and more support now in erecting a dam against the 'mòr-shruth na Beurla'. Most of them realise this, and realise too that it is not enough merely to use the 'language of the outlaw' like their compeers of former ages, they must also recreate and reshape it.

Hamish Henderson (Seumas mac Eanruig)

To Christopher Murray Grieve (Hugh MacDiarmid), 1 March 1948

Dear Chris

I've hitchhiked to England to tear the guts out of *Our Time* for failing to print your Lenin page and Mike [Grieve]'s Gyndagooster.

Here I find there's been a new Thermidor – Holbrook and Manifold have been liquidated, and a cadaverous school-marmy Czech called Jellinck reigns in their stead!

Whether I've got to be a new Barras, and wield the sword of Vendémiaire is not quite clear yet. Anyway I got cracking on this cove Jellinck, and the result has been gratifying. He's agreed to do a complete Scottish number of *Our Time* in the spring or early summer – containing a Lenin page twice as long, a full-length article by myself on the Scottish renaissance, an article (? by MacDougall) on John Maclean, a study of Lewis Grassic Gibbon (? by yourself), plus stories, poems etc. *And* Gyndagooster! I also sold him a copy of the Ballads.

By Christ, if I'd added an article by Valda on you I swear by all things heroic he'd have accepted it!

Running in London now is *The Gorbals Story* (see enclosure) a *succès fou*. It's not all *that* good, which is eloquent of the depths to which the English stage has sunk.

I enclose a poem by [E.P.] Thompson (son of the Edward you knew), who's now living in Wester Ross. Write to him and make contact. (Maybe it would do for the *Voice.*) Anyway he's a worthwhile contact, for he'll be a power yet in the C.P.

Yesterday I got a terrible letter from Heinz describing winter in Duisburg, and deaths from freezing in the cellars of that ruined shambles. A pity it didn't come earlier – it would have done very well as a supplement to my German article ['Germany in Defeat' I & II, *Voice of Scotland,* 1948].

The *Voice* sells out in Cambridge and Collets London – I'm convinced the circulation could be increased tenfold.

Love to Valda
    Yours ever,
        Hamish
PS: *The Swordsman* is on here. I'm going along for a laugh.

To the SCOTSMAN, 15 May 1948

Sir – Few contributors to this unenlightening correspondence seem to have grasped the fundamental questions at issue. Allow me to give some direction to the debate by making one or two necessary points.

Firstly: the reason why the Makars are so boisterously assailed by all and sundry is not primarily because they write in Lallans, but because they form an *avant garde.* One need hardly point out that an *avant garde* as such is traditionally suspect. Keats, for example, would consider the present correspondence as merely so much matey badinage: in his day he had to take infinitely worse slangings. In fact, Byron's celebrated line about Keats being killed off "by one critique" (and an Edinburgh critique at that!) had a certain degree of truth in it.

Secondly, the language the Makars use is looked upon as archaic, not because it has ceased to be spoken, but because it is no longer the 'done thing' to speak it. If some of the critics of Lallans writers had been con-scripted into the Royal Scots Fusiliers or the Cameronians they would pretty quickly have altered their ideas about the vitality of spoken Scots.

Thirdly, Lallans poems *have* been translated into English, and most, granted any sensibility on the part of the reader, can be immediately apprehended as poetry. The following is a prose version of Hugh Mac-Diarmid's famous poem 'The Eemis Stane': "In the very dead of the cold harvest night the world, like a loose tombstone, sways in the sky, and my eerie memories fall like a down-drive of snow. Like a down-drive of snow so that I cannot read the words cut on the stone, even if the moss of fame and the lichen of history had not overgrown them."

I submit that the above prose translation although it cannot hope by its very nature to recapture the sonorous yet subtle beauty of the Scots, is nevertheless adequate proof that one is dealing here with a poem of the first order. Another thing about it which leaps to the eye is that it is in the 'modern' idiom, having far more in common with the poetry of Jouve and Montale than with that of, say, Walter de la Mare. Furthermore, it makes as bold and imaginative a use of Scots as Eliot has made of English.

After countless inroads the old Scots tongue now stands like a great ruined broch, with the rubble of centuries lying round it. Stones from that rubble have for too long gone to nothing higher than the building of dykes around lowly kailyairds. In poems like 'The Eemis Stane' an attempt has at last been made to put stone on stone, to rebuild the tower. Is it strange that modern Scottish poets, the heirs of Dunbar and Henryson, should consider this task well worthy of their labours?

Of course they may fail. Possibly they are not equal to the task. But history will at any rate give them credit for bringing the Scottish cultural predicament ruthlessly into the light of day.

I am &c – Hamish Henderson

TO C. M. GRIEVE, 2 MAY 1950

Dear Chris

Thanks for the poems. The only ones now missing are: the one on Edinburgh from *Lucky Poet*, and 'If There Are Bounds To Any Man' (*Second Hymn to Lenin*)[1].

I am working hard on Antonio Gramsci's *Letters from Prison*, a book of the first importance. [Gramsci] was certainly the most important Marxist thinker outside Russia in the period 1920–1935. His *Machiavelli and the Modern State* (just published) is a book which will certainly take its place among Marxist classics.

What you tell me about the Irish number is not very encouraging. Remember this, that the work of collecting material was started over a year ago in full agreement with yourself. If the Irish number fails to come out, our name will be mud all over green Erin. This will not help the Scottish cause in any way that I can see.[2]

Please put one or two numbers of *The Nationalist* in the post for me, as well as the copies of *the Voice*. I'd like to see what way the wee breath of Wilkie wind is now blowing.

All the best to Valda & Mike,

Yours

Hamish

PS: If Kenny decides not to produce the Irish number, get the material from him and get another printer to produce it. I think I can maybe borrow enough dough to cover the expenses – H.

TO H. H. FROM EWAN MACCOLL, 16 FEBRUARY 1951

Dear Hamish

Just a brief note – there is a character wandering around this sceptred isle at the moment, named Alan Lomax. He is a Texan and none the worse for that, he is also just about the most important name in American folk-

---

1. The Scottish Committee of the Communist Party proposed publishing a selection of MacDiarmd's poetry, edited by Henderson. This never appeared.
2. *Voice of Scotland* Irish number, edited by Henderson, which never appeared.

song circles. He is over here with a super recording unit and a girl, Robin Roberts, who sings like an angel. Columbia Gramophone Co. are financing his trip. The idea is that he will record the folk-singers of a group of countries (he has already covered Africa – America – the West Indies – the central European countries). And Columbia will produce an album of discs – an hour for each country. He is not interested in trained singers or refined versions of the folksongs. He wants to record traditional-style singers doing ballads, work songs, political satires etc. It occurred to me that you could help him in two ways.

1   Record some of your soldier songs and any other songs you know. You sang some to me in the little cafe opposite the Epworth Hall.

2   Introduce him to other Scots folk-singers.

You know the kind of thing he wants: bothy songs, street songs, soldier songs, [?march] music, the big Gaelic stuff, weavers' and miners' songs, etc.

This is important, Hamish. It is vital that Scotland is well represented in this collection. It would be fatal if the 'folksy' boys were to cash in.

If you can help, write to him – Alan Lomax, c/o BBC, London. He intends coming to Scotland in about a week's time.

Do try and help.

Yours aye, Ewan

PS: If and why you meet him, get him to sing some of his American coal miners' songs. They are terrific.

TO H.H. FROM ALAN LOMAX, 20 SEPTEMBER 1951

Dear Hamish Henderson

I've been travelling the roads of the world, hitting the high places and the low places, the rough and the smooth, for about twenty years, recording folksongs and ballads from all sorts of people, but I have never had such a kind and warm-hearted treatment from anywhere as from the people of Scotland, and I just wanted to write you this letter and tell you how much I appreciated this. It makes all kinds of difference when you're a long way from home, to be treated like you were a member of the family.

What you have done, however, is to help the folksongs of your country to be better known. Thank you for your songs, which will be listened to by scholars and just ordinary people with the greatest interest and pleasure.

The people of Scotland recorded about 25 hours of their folksongs this summer. The whole set will go to the University of Edinburgh folklore archive for the permanent benefit of the Scottish people. Some will go to the BBC Permanent Records library, and some will be published by the Columbia Recording Company in New York City, and some will be used in my BBC broadcasts. And all will be deposited in a museum in the USA. No use will be made of the records by me without first obtaining your written permission.

'Tail Toddle' and 'Wap and Row' of the folklore you recorded for me is being incorporated in the album of Scots folksongs I am preparing for publication by Columbia Recording Company in the States this year. There is a money order for the token fee paid for your permission to permit Columbia to put this Folklore of the Scots Album in the World Library of Folk Music. This does not limit any other use you make of it. I hope you will be as generous with the next collector as you have been with me.

Please sigh the attached form and return it to me,

Yours cordially,
Alan Lomax

TO MARIAN SUGDEN, 29 NOVEMBER 1951

Dear Marian

There's an Alan Lomax programme on Tuesday called *I Heard Scotland Sing* (Sc. Home Service, and I think London regional too, at 8pm). Listen in to it – it's really good. A lot of the singers took part in the People's Festival ceilidh I told you about. Highlights: Mary Morrison (of Barra) mimicking the pipes in superb mouth-music. Jimmy MacBeath the tinker-singer discussing Shakespeare's *Macbeth*, and a ceilidh we had up in Aberdeenshire during which I sang 'Tail Toddle'! Also bits from the People's Festival Ceilidh.

From 1 January I shall be on a three-month tour of the north financed by the School of Scottish Studies, Edin. University, collecting ballads and finding singers. God's own job – and hospitality money provided. The truth is that the University people were so impressed by Lomax's achievements (the amount of fine singing we collected in a short time clear bowled 'em over) that they've disregarded my suspect politics at long last and offered me a job!

Mica male! About time too. (The 'hospitality money' means that I'm entitled to put down as expenses the occasional drop of the immortal cratur for adding the edge to fiddle tune or song.)

> And sae at last this bonnie cat
> he had a stroke o' luck...

The Gramsci position is the same as before, it appears. Bloody annoying.

All the best to you both (and regards to maters, paters etc.)

Love, Hamish

TO THE *SCOTSMAN*, 9 FEBRUARY 1953

Sir – Your correspondent, Mr. A.J. Aitken, has summed up the linguistic problems facing Scotland with admirable lucidity. May I add one or two points, by way of amplifying and documenting his general line of argument?

That upper-class English speech is very unlike Scottish speech is obvious. What is less often realised is that the dialects of North Oxford and South Kensington have altered a great deal in this present century, and that certain features of these dialects which to an educated Scot have all the appearance of linguistic abuses have become more common even in the last ten years or so. The intrusive 'r' is an obvious example: it was heard much less frequently in the speech of BBC announcers before the war than it is today.

Fifty or sixty years ago the phrase 'at home' was pronounced in southern English very much as it was pronounced by Scots school masters (although the 'h' tended to be elided, and not only by 'Cockneys'.) Nowadays a very usual pronunciation of this phrase is something like 'et heowm', an attempt to ape the prestige speech of Oxford and the English public schools. This tendency is carried to absurdity and (for Scots at least) to nausea in the 'refained speech' of certain pathetic creatures both north and south of the border who imagine that they are counterfeiting a 'good-class accent'.

Realisation that southern English speech is in a period of fairly rapid transition cannot fail to illuminate the plight of BBC announcers in Scotland. It is claimed that they are all conversant with the 'guid Scots tongue'. This may be so, but it is very difficult to move straight from a language in which, as in Italian, every part of the vocal apparatus is called into play.

One word to Mr Aitken. He is wrong if he thinks I want to 'impose' a granite-hard standard of Scottish-English speech. I went out of my way to emphasise that I want a flexible line which would encourage regionalisms. But in order to counter the present policy of forcible anglicisation we must draw the line somewhere.

Let me put it like this. If an announcer pronounces Boer War with the accent of Barra or the accent of Buchan, fair enough, but if he pronounces Boer War as if he were a Pekingese barking defiance (baw waw! baw waw!), he should be out on his neck.

I am &c – Hamish Henderson

TO THE *SCOTSMAN*, 17 FEBRUARY 1953

Sir – When I referred to the tape-recordings of Scots folksong housed in the archives of the School of Scottish Studies as a "reference library", I certainly did not mean to imply that this was their only function. I only meant that where Scottish linguistic problems are concerned they constitute a court of appeal considerably more reliable than the average textbook.

It would be a great irony if your readers assumed that I did not want my recordings of Scots folksong to be broadcast. On the contrary, I believe that the broadcasting of them would be an event of great cultural significance in Scotland.

The decision as to whether or not they should be broadcast does not, however, rest with me. It rests, I need hardly say, with the BBC and with the School of Scottish Studies, which owns the tapes.

It is possible that either one or both of these organisations may oppose the broadcasting of the great traditional songs which I have collected, but I consider it very unlikely. These songs lie near the heart of the older Scottish tradition; they are beyond doubt the genuine article as preserved and sung by people to whom it is still a living part of reality. As for the quality of performance, it has been described by individuals well qualified to judge – for example, Professor S.T.M. Newman, Dr Herbert Wiseman, and Mr William Montgomerie – as on the whole exceedingly high.

One of the functions of a university is surely to inspire the people. And what is the most reasonable function of a broadcasting system if it is not to entertain the people (and provide them *viva voce* with some stimulating food for thought)? I cannot imagine a project in which these various aims and functions could be more happily combined than in the broadcasting of genuine Scots folksong to the Scottish people.

The singers, I might add, are all for it: they fail to see why second-rate performances and battered 'lyric gems' should monopolise the air for ever.

Needless to say, they seldom clear the hurdle. Even when announcing the names of the tunes in programmes of Scottish dance music they usually pronounce the Scots words as if they were speaking a foreign language for which they felt a slight distaste. I often wish they could somehow get relayed back to them the vivid comments of a certain Aberdeenshire folk-singer who makes his croft ring with Doric [orig. Lallans] abuse at moments such as these.

It is not so long back since I heard 'The Muckin o Geordie's Byre' referred to as "The Meukin of Jawdie's Beye-a" – the most gruesome bloodbath of vowels that ever savaged a living language!

What is the solution? The BBC has a great opportunity. If it rose to the occasion it could arrest the process of wholesale anglicisation, and give fresh dignity and currency, not only to Gaelic and Lallans, but also to the traditional Scots-English of an older generation: an infinitely more pleasing speech, I may say, than the usual run of announcers' English. What is needed is an accepted standard of Scots-English pronunciation – not a hard and fast standard, but a flexible line which would permit, and indeed encourage, deviations to Highland and Lowland. If we could get provisional agreement on the need for this – and the correspondence in your columns shows that there is widespread feeling in favour of such a move – we would shortly find, I think, that other parts of the English-speaking world would increasingly come to accept it as a standard. (I am thinking especially of the northern English of Tyne, Humber and Tees, who would certainly prefer Scots-English to the Hampstead-Surbiton variety.)

The Italians say that the best Italian is *lingua toscana in bocca romana* (the Tuscan speech on Roman lips). Could we not have a shot at proving that the best English is *lingua inglese in bocca scozzese*?

It may be objected that we would have difficulty in agreeing on a standard. I do not think that there are any formidable obstacles. Use might well be made of the tape recordings in the archives of the School of Scottish Studies of Edinburgh University, which are not only an incomparable treasure-house of the folksong of our country, as preserved by real folksingers, but also a linguistic reference library of the first importance.

I am &c – Hamish Henderson

Flower and Iron of the Truth
A Survey of Contemporary Scottish Writing

Hamish Henderson

In the first decade of this century Scotland presented a daunting spectacle of cultural ruin. To many observers it seemed unlikely that the country could much longer maintain even a façade of national identity. The English imperialist Ascendancy had consolidated itself, with the full acquiescence of the Scottish bourgeoisie, during the course of the nineteenth century, and its domination in academic circles was virtually complete. The indigenous traditions of the people, both Gaelic and Lallans, seemed to have been left tattered and defenceless before the big battalions of alien aggression.

This apparent abdication was merely underlined by the blowsy vocal patriotism of the Scottish burgesses. These vied with each other in extolling the beauties of a countryside they had savaged, and in eulogising the works of a poet whose poems they no longer properly understood.

Yet today, as even hostile critics are obliged to admit, the picture is quite different. Although the "official" crust of anglicising authority is still very much in evidence, forces have emerged in the last twenty-five years vigorous enough to change the whole atmosphere of Scottish life. A generation of younger poets and intellectuals has grown up which would be the just pride of any country in Europe. Let us examine more fully this curious phenomenon.

In the first place, the cultural revival cannot be disassociated from the growth to political maturity of the Scottish working class during World War I. In the great campaign against increased rents in the first years of the war and in the mass fights against conscription from 1916 onwards, the Scottish people rediscovered an élan which had carried it into action in 1848 and in the Crofters' War. And it threw up a leader of genius, the Glasgow schoolmaster John Maclean, of whose indomitable battle in the interests of the workers Gallacher has written so movingly in *Revolt on the Clyde*, and to whose revolutionary inspiration Lenin himself paid tribute. It would be hard to overestimate Maclean's service to Scotland: not only did he use his profound knowledge of Marxism to train a whole generation of activists, not only did he transform the workers' struggle in the industrial belt of Scotland and make the Clyde an embattled outpost of the European proletariat—he also, by a correct interpretation of the national problem, showed the workers and crofters of our country that the Scottish past was their rightful heritage.

Understanding from his own background and from his parents' stories the reality of the class war in the Highlands, he recalled to the people such episodes from their recent history as the Land League, and such documents as the following manifesto of Highland resistance:

"The enemy is the landlord, the agent, the capitalist—and the Parliament which makes and maintains inhuman and iniquitous laws.

"Cut down the telegraph wires and posts, carry away the wires and instruments! Stop the mailcarts, destroy the letters.

"Burn the property of all obnoxious landlords and agents. Set fire to the heather to destroy the game: disturb the deer: poison game-dogs!

"The oppressed toilers of England and the millions of disinherited people are watching your actions. Their hearts are with you in your battle for right and liberty.

"*God save the people!*"

The achievement of Maclean was almost as great in the field of culture as it was in the field of active struggle. The legend of him was beyond question one of the principal formative influences which went to shape Hugh MacDiarmid, the giant of the Scottish Renaissance. MacDiarmid's *Hymns to Lenin* are in a certain sense his own tribute to Maclean, and many of the younger poets influenced by him have celebrated Scotland's greatest revolutionary figure in lyrics and ballads. Among these are Sydney Goodsir Smith, John Kincaid, Maurice Blythman ("Thurso Berwick"), and the Gaelic poet Sorley MacLean.

In the second place, Scotland, having played an important rôle in this international movement, began once again to look at Europe and to feel herself part of it. The manifest intellectual indigence of the great bulk of "conforming" pro-English Ascendancy wowsers in the Scottish universities increasingly alienated the livelier spirits in Scottish academic life, and brought about between the wars a re-orientation of our intellectual contacts in the direction of the continent—a resumption, therefore, of the traditional Scottish alignments which had tended to be forgotten during the course of the nineteenth century. Thus it could come about that MacDiarmid was translating Blok and Rilke years before the "New Signatures" group in Oxford made such a song and dance about "discovering" them. Gradually an intellectual climate came into being which favoured still more interesting experiments, and eventually Douglas Young could present in Scottish dress the verse of a dozen assorted languages.

The doyen of the Scottish movement is a Borderer, Hugh MacDiarmid. This redoubtable adversary of reaction in literature and in life has exerted an incalculable influence on the development of letters north of the Cheviots. A poet of the first order in Lallans, a coruscating polemicist in English and (for the last decade) an intrepid explorer with his own plastic multilingo, he has served as a rallying point for every forward-looking movement in the country since the publication of *Sangschaw* in 1925. Rescuing the Scots tongue from the slough of havering provincialism into which it had fallen, he demonstrated incontrovertibly by his own example that it was still capable of carrying art poetry: his *Drunk Man Looks At A Thistle*, a masterpiece which with unique bravado mixed a score of glorious lyrics with pantagruelian dollops of audacious philosophical banter, set the seal on this achievement.

For the benefit of readers not conversant with Lallans, here is a prose translation into English of the 'Eemis Stane', one of the early lyrics which remain his most celebrated poems—unreasonably, perhaps, because they were followed by "the magnificent *To Circumjack Cencrastus* and the sweeping majesty of the *Hymns to Lenin*" (Lewis Grassic Gibbon):

> *In the very dead of the cold harvest night the world like a loose tomb-stone sways in the sky, and my eerie memories fall like a downdrive of snow.*
>
> *Like a downdrive of snow, so that I could not see the words cut out in the stone—even if the moss of fame and the lichen of history had not overgrown them.*

This revelation of the potentialities of the "auld leid" had an effect on his younger contemporaries that one can properly call electric. But MacDiarmid's most positive service does not lie in his championship of the Scots language: it is rather to be found in the single-minded devotion he has shown in furthering the great cause of the proletariat in Scotland, and in clarifying the relation of the cultural revival to the political struggle. He realised clearly, and stressed over and over again that no literary revival is worth a damn if it fails to identify itself with the *present* difficulties and tasks of the people. And conversely, that no poetry which desires to be actual can afford to neglect the ramifications of exploit and dream in the people's past. In short, that Scottish poetry, if it is to contribute anything of value to the international complex, must first of all throw off the alien mummy-wrappings we have heard of, and recover its true identity.

MacDiarmid's stand in defence of these ideas against every kind of defamation and calumny has been little short of heroic. Now, having won through, he towers in rugged monolithic eminence above the contemporary Scottish scene.

The poets that have followed MacDiarmid's lead can be divided for convenience's sake into two schools. The first includes those poets known as the "Lallans Makars"—Albert Mackie, Sydney Goodsir Smith, Maurice Lindsay and Douglas Young. These are all considerable artists, and one of them (Sydney Smith, author of *The Devil's Waltz* and *Under the Eildon Tree*) is a poet of real power. Although their work shows pronounced differences, they have one major aim in common: a desire to extend and enrich the capacities of the revitalised Scots tongue as a vehicle for literature. Hence, constituting themselves a kind of unofficial Academy, they have done useful spadework in a number of fields, such as the standardisation of Lallans spelling; they have also joined issue polemically with the literary reaction. One of their company, Maurice Lindsay, has performed a function rather similar to that of Allan Ramsay in the eighteenth century: an indefatigable editor and anthologist, he has succeeded in making the Scottish public definitely Lallans-conscious.

The second of the two schools I referred to is gradually emerging. The poets belonging to it are not primarily interested in the language question, though they have turned one by one from English to Scots or Gaelic. They are resolved to carry a stage further MacDiarmid's application of Marxism to the Scottish predicament, and are eager to produce work which will interpret more immediately the reality of the Scottish people—of the commons of Alba, the industrial proletariat, the dockers, miners and shipyard workers, the Highland remnant. In a word, they have comprehended the need for a literature of *presentification*. Reacting strongly against the seeming archaism of the Makars—an archaism more of subject-matter than of language—they lay at their door the tendency of the Scottish public to equate Lallans poetry with a predilection for the grotesque: a taking wing on Jamieson's battered broomstick to riotous, non-stop Walpurgisnacht.

The poets of this second school (sometimes called the Clyde Group) want more Maclean and less Mahoun[1] in Scottish poetry. They are inclined to ask (and the question is relevant) what contact Lindsay's "lanely wishan-wells" are supposed to have with the reality of life in Govan or Hamilton—or for that matter with the reality of life in Comrie or Lochboisdale. Conscious of the enormous untapped potentialities of Scots poetry, they fear that, left to the Mahoun-mongers, it may turn into a mere academic exercise, a field for Alexandrian virtuosity—a "pluralism of superstructures" above a a life with which it has lost all contact. And therefore they are in a mood to give Mahoun a kick on his ample dowp that will send him limping out of Lallans verse for a twelvemonth.

One of the most interesting of these writers is John Kincaid, whose *Setterday Nicht Symphonie* has just been published by the Caledonian Press. This poem comes nearer than anything I have yet seen to a successful evocation of the beauty that can be struck from the forbidding grey whinstone of Glasgow tenement life.

> Ay, birl awa citie, mak a gob at the mune,
> fling a haunfu o' stars at the heids o' the priests,
> tak the Clyde i' your airms...
> Ay citie, ma citie, skirl awa citie,
> skretch oot your lauchin til waas faain doon;
> your flair is aa stampin wi' lads an' wi' lasses
> wi' joy i' their banes an' daunce i' their bluid.
> > O citie, ma citie
> > to Freedom be leal!
> > Tak haud o' the nicht!
> > Wha's for a quadrille?

Kincaid calls Glasgow "ma douce raucle citie." In the startling juxtaposition of these two untranslatable Scots words one recognises the brilliant single phrase that one was waiting for... Another of the Clyde Group who promises well is Kincaid's friend and comrade "Thurso Berwick". This young writer has produced several love poems which show great insight and tenderness. The best of these is 'The Twa Wynds', published in the March *Voice of Scotland*. He has also written some excellent satirical verse.

The Caledonian Press has to its credit furthermore the publication of *Whit Tyme in the Day*, which is the first book of a difficult but (I think) rewarding poet, T.S. Law.

---

1. Mahoun: One of the many names for that darling of Scottish literature—the Devil.

A poet who is, and will probably remain, difficult to place is Alexander Scott. This young Aberdonian who has just been appointed Lecturer in Scottish Language and Literature in the University of Glasgow has a grasp of the living rhythms and idiom of the Scots speech markedly superior to that of most of his brother makars. In addition, his work shows a careful craftsmanship too often lacking in Lallans verse. A selection of his writing will appear later this year in the Saltire Society's poetry series.

Space forbids mention of more than the names of several important figures whose work has attracted attention both north and south of the border: William Soutar (whose death deprived Scotland of one of its best twentieth century poets), William Jeffrey, Edwin Muir, G.S. Fraser, Norman McCaig, J.F. Hendry, Adam Drinan, Ruthven Todd, George Bruce and the two best-known Gaelic poets, Sorley MacLean and George Campbell Hay. All of these deserve separate articles to themselves. Likewise, as far as the theatre is concerned, I cannot do more than draw the attention of the reader to Montague Slater's article on Glasgow Unity in the July *Our Time*, and mention in addition the names of Robert MacLellan, Ewan MacColl and Robert Kemp. The most interesting novels since the death of Lewis Grassic Gibbon are Fionn MacColla's *And the Cock Crew* and Naomi Mitchison's *The Bull Calves*.

Enough has been said to show that things are moving in Scotland. In all the arts the scene has been transformed, and as most of the writers referred to are young, one can safely say that a wonderful *Blueteperiode* of Scottish letters is in its opening stages. But the most encouraging sign is the fact that, as in Italy and Latin America, the majority of the poets, artists and intellectuals are of the Left. That they are also Scots, proudly conscious of their country's past and its separate identity and tradition, stands to reason. Scotland has suffered too terribly in her own body the fury of the modern crisis to be ignorant of the vital issues involved—and these include national survival. Nevertheless in the international field her alignment has never been in doubt, and if it comes to the issue she will certainly prove this. As Hugh MacDiarmid wrote almost twenty years ago in the *First Hymn to Lenin* (a poem with the "unheard-of simplicity" of Neruda's *Songs to Stalingrad*):

> But now in the flower and iron of the truth
> to you we turn—and turn in vain nae mair.
> Ilka fule has folly eneuch for sadness—
> but now we are wise, an' wi' wisdom tear
> the veil o' being: and are face to face
> wi' the human race.

Note: This essay was first published in the left-wing weekly *Our Time*, September 10th 1948. Henderson persuaded the new editors to publish a Scottish feature, which he edited himself, to coincide with the John Maclean Memorial Rally that November. The issue also included an article on Lewis Grassic Gibbon by MacDiarmid, as well as his 'Common Riding'; poems celebrating Maclean by his namesake Sorley, and Sydney Goodsir Smith; and George Campbell Hay's poem 'Lomsgrios na Tire' ('Destruction of the Land'). This article, written when Henderson was 28, and appearing in the same year as his *Elegies*, represents the moment when he was closest to MacDiarmid, while at the same time simultaneously signalling the break that would come in the next decade – Alec Finlay

Scots Language in Transition

Some thoughts arising from Hamish Henderson's essay 'Flower and Iron of the Truth'

Angus Calder

I was reading Irvine Welsh's *Marabou Stork Nightmares* (Jonathan Cape, 1995) when I came to the point on page 25 where the narrator's father is planning to emigrate to South Africa:

> I didnae really ken whether or no I wanted to go. It was just eftir that that I lit my first really big fire. I'd always liked fires. Boney nights were the best night of the year in the scheme, Guy Fawkes because you got fireworks, but Victoria Day n aw. We'd go down the beach tae get wood or find other boneys in the scheme and raid them. Sometimes, though, we got raided ourselves. You would get cudgels and stanes and try to defend your bonfire against raiders. There was always fights with stanes in the scheme. The first thing I learned tae dae was to fling a stane.

Something was worrying me. It's clear enough that the narrator, hospitalised in a coma, reverts frequently in his mind from a "grown up" standard English voice to the Muirhouse speech of his childhood. But Welsh's presentation of this form of Scots seems inconsistent. It's not just that the syntax is tidied up; the spelling and vocabulary seem to swither on no fixed principle from Tom Leonard-esque transliteration of 'bad' speech ("n aw") to standard modified only by one's prior sense of a non-standard voicing ("try to defend your bonfire against raiders" – why not "boney" this time?)

Then I decided I needn't worry. I will come back to this.

Hamish Henderson's 'Flower and Iron of the Truth' is now dated, but this is not to its discredit at all. A committed writer must be topical and all urgently topical writing dates. Byron's wonderful assault on Southey in his *Vision of Judgement* is thoroughly dated, though still valid in its polemical thrust. My interest centres on what Henderson states and implies about Scots language in his essay. But before moving on to that I feel constrained to remind you what sort of year 1948 was.

Henderson, and a high proportion of his readers, had been engaged in a bloody and often barbaric war. The victors had cause to construe it as epic. In alliance with the unbelievably brave and tenacious Soviet peoples, and with partisans in Europe who also seemed to represent the dawning strength of world Communism, Scottish warriors had helped to overthrow the evil right-wing regimes of Hitler, Mussolini and Tojo.

Neruda is still generally recognised as a very great poet, but I doubt if anyone on earth now regards his *Songs to Stalingrad* as a masterpiece. MacDiarmid's *Hymns to Lenin*, despite wonderful passages, now generate some embarrassment. Everyone should realise that William Gallacher, in his book *Revolt on the Clyde,* cynically co-opted John Maclean's memory to the cause of the Communist Party of Great Britain when, in reality, back in the early 1920s, Maclean's refusal to join that party had prompted Gallacher himself to put it about that the man was "mentally unbalanced and suffering from hallucinations". But in the moment of anti-Fascist triumph, when it seemed nevertheless that the USA, waging cold war, might promote right-wing reaction and restoration everywhere, it was inevitable that Henderson should hail Gallacher and Maclean, Neruda and MacDiarmid, as leaders and prophets for the workers of the world.

Where, though, could he and should he place the cause of Scots language (and Gaelic) in "the struggle"? Henderson's essay shows that already, in 1948, the Scots lyrics of MacDiarmid published quarter of a century before were clearly seen as the launchpad for a rocketing revival – "rescuing the Scots tongue from the slough of havering provincialism into which it has fallen." However, his demurral that MacDiarmid's "most positive service does not lie in his championship of the Scots language" but in his "single-minded devotion" to the proletarian cause indicates how the imperatives, as he saw them, of 1948, must push Henderson himself to discriminate between "committed" and "uncommitted" uses of Scots. His tribute to the "considerable" artistry of the poets – Mackie, Goodsir Smith, Lindsay and Young – whom he groups as "Lallans Makars" is tepid. His praise of the "Clyde Group" – a shadowy presence at the most in our current assessment of twentieth century Scottish culture – is based on their recognition of the need for a "a literature of *presentification*": they are not interested in the niceties of the language question, but in the here and now of proletarian struggle.

There are awkwardnesses in Henderson's line of argument which, in effect, he himself later acknowledged. It is not clear that the campaign for Scottish nationhood implies a need for the revival of Lallans. Even if it does, nationalism itself is not necessarily, in Marxist terms, "progressive". The Left has as its primary objective the arousal of the working class, and the genteel Lallans of Maurice Lindsay will hardly serve that purpose. Internationalism is essential, so it may be more important to read Gramsci than Dunbar, Sartre than Hogg. "Facts are chiels that winna ding", and if the workers don't want Lallans, "academic" exercises in "Alexandrian virtuosity" are pointless.

MacDiarmid himself, by 1948, had long turned away from Lallans, or any form of Scots. Alan Bold (*MacDiarmid*, John Murray, 1988) attributes the shift to the poet's move to Whalsay in 1933. "He wanted an erudite alternative, an English capable of articulating his understanding of a world stripped to its essentials; he felt his internal struggle for survival was externalised in the loneliest reaches of the Shetland landscape." He evolved a "Synthetic English", stiff with technical and scientific terms, for his great poem *On a Raised Beach*. Thereafter, despite his angry reaction against Edwin Muir's dismissal of Scots as useless now for serious verse, the main current of MacDiarmid's work flowed in English.

Henderson's own relationship with MacDiarmid would become fraught and complex. Nowhere in his own verse does one detect overweening influence from the older poet. Henderson's magnificent *Elegies for the*

Dead in Cyrenaica (also published in 1948) are in English, but the idiom seems heavily affected, like some of MacDiarmid's work, by conscious-ness of Gaelic. No English soldier of Henderson's generation wrote anything like them, yet they do relate to the Gaelic poems by Sorley Maclean, also from the desert war. Henderson showed that one could be intensely "Scottish" with the lexicon of standard English.

On the other hand, the language of the oral tradition which Henderson, as collector, would build into the base of the Scottish Folk Revival, came to him, as living utterance, exactly as whatever it was. Jeannie Robertson sang the great ballads with deep respect, but their language existed for her in a continuum with her own everyday speech, and she did not theorise at all about whether her north-eastern tongue was "correct Scots", nor give a damn about how words should be spelt. If contemporary urban songs were written by those engaged in the Revival they would work only if people in pubs could identify with their language. Lallans poetry had a kind of heyday in the 1940s and 1950s with the writers whom Henderson mentions in 'Flower and Iron'. But it did not connect with the Revival, nor with a new Scottish way of doing theatre which evolved by the 1970s as (one might whimsically put it) a belated offspring of the pre-war marriage of Ewan McColl to the Englishwoman Joan Littlewood, whose post-Brechtian practice in East London influenced John McGrath. By the 1970s, indeed, Lallans verse mostly looked as provincial and politically inert as Scots in general had been when MacDiarmid had launched his Renaissance. (The sadly late Tom Scott was a significant exception.)

Yet now, in the 1990s, writing in Scots is arguably richer and more wide-ranging than it has been for centuries. Moving back towards Irvine Welsh I ask myself, what does "writing in Scots" mean?

Henderson's 1948 article refers, rather mysteriously, to the Lallans Makars as the Mahoun school, as if he saw self-conscious *diablerie* as a prime motive in their writing. But self-conscious versifying in Scots in recent years has suggested a different, less perky cognomen – "the Aiblins School." The word "aiblins", never heard, at least by me, in the streets and pubs of Glasgow and Edinburgh, typifies the "Alexandrian" or "Parnassian" artificiality of the version of Scots favoured by purists. It can induce exquisite mental (or even, at public readings, physical) torture – "aiblins" this and "aiblins" yon, and all too often some paranoid nationalistic whinge providing the verse with predictable content.

Nevertheless, I repeat, writing in Scots flourishes. How can this be? The Folk Revival may partly account for it. Robin Hall and Jimmie Macgregor on TV, the Corries in concert, may not have been the finest exponents of the Scots words they sang, but their vitality and charisma led the songs safely away from parlour gentility back towards the pubs and school playgrounds. TV, again, came to provide a market for drama using "regional" voices, including Scots. If the effect of pre-war radio had been to standardise English, in the TV era of *Coronation Street* difference was reasserted. In the last resort, though, literary influence is likely to weigh most on writers, and they were likely to respond to the power of Scots as used by MacDiarmid and Grassic Gibbon even if they didn't care to theorise about the language or check their spelling against approved forms.

The growing self-confidence of Scottish culture has provided writers with reassurance that their own way of doing things is probably okay.

For a respectable example of "Alexandrian" verse in Scots we need look not further than Maurice Lindsay's 'Hurlygush', title poem of a volume published, as it happens, in 1948:

> The hurlygush and hallyoch o the watter
> skinklan i the moveless simmer sun
> harles aff the scourie mountain wi a yatter
> that thru ten-thoosan centuries has run.

Collected Poems 1940–1990, Aberdeen University Press 1990, p.19

The basis of this poem is a structure of feeling which corresponds to English Georgianism. Timeless, pastoral subject matter is presented in light quatrains. As with that forerunner of Georgianism, Housman, such verse in Scots may make overt classical reference. 'The Shepherd's Dochter' whom Douglas Young saw buried in Fife in 1949 inspired a fine poem, but one which is pastoral in the most precise sense of that word; and as a classicist by profession, Young knew exactly what he was up to, where his cypresses came from:

> The murners skail, thankfu tae lea thon place
> whaur the blythest, bonniest lass liggs i the mouls.
> Lent lilies loup and cypresses stand stieve...

As Henderson points out in his 1948 article, the versatile Young "could present in Scottish dress the verse of a dozen assorted languages", and the aptness of Scots as an alternative to English in translation has often since been tested and confirmed. But with the wholly original verse of the generation whom Henderson calls Lallans Makars we are left wondering, as we don't after reading MacDiarmid's *Drunk Man*, whether Scots is more than an unusual flavour added to old recipes.

Henderson does not mention Robert Garioch, whose stuffy Edinburgh demotic could not be attainted for archaism or fake *diablerie*:

> I saw him comin out the N.B. Grill,
> creashy and winey, wi his famous voice
> crackin some comic bawr to please three choice
> notorious bailies, lauchan fit to kill...

Collected Poems, Macdonald 1977, p.125

But 'Glisk of the Great', as a sonnet, represents Garioch's habit of applying fresh, vivid Scots to traditional forms. The result isn't at all foosty or Alexandrian, but it roots him in traditional, learned continuities which younger writers such as Morgan and even MacCaig, were concerned to pass beyond, into freer verse forms.

Effective verse in various Scots voices is still produced in traditional metres. But the Lallans offensive has petered out, if by Lallans is meant a single, standard Scots tongue synthesised for literary purposes. Take, for instance, Robert Alan Jamieson's debut volume, *Shoormal* (Polygon, 1986) containing poems in what we outsiders might call Shetlandic, but he calls Norrøna/Scots. Jamieson remarks in his introduction that "Whilst the poems in Norrøna/Scots may be artificial, their language is still more natural to my tongue than that of those in English." 'Song oda Post War Exiles' is perhaps the most accessible of these poems. A couple are leaving their small island for a "cooncilhoose in Scallwa" (the relative metropolis, Scalloway!) The wife is eager to go, her man grieves:

> Dat last faent glisk o wir croft de da shore,
> Aa quhite-washed clean, brukk gien fae da door,
> I'll never forgit it, I canna forgit it,
> For days an nichts hit's wi me alaek
> Dat last rummlt stane I touched or wir daek,
> Dat last faent glisk as I pulled on da oar,
> Aa quhite-washed clean, brukk gien fae da door.
> Hit med me greet t'see it.

Whatever (admitted) artificiality there may be in an idiom which Jamieson himself calls "a synthetic Shetlandic using some Norn words and phrases bound together with Scots", it is emphatically not Alexandrian Lallans artificiality. The aim is not to represent a revived tradition but to give voice idiosyncratically to the experience of living in a particular place within Scotland's territory at a particular time.

W.N. Herbert is another young writer who, in the 1980s, came up with a non-Lallans rationale for his own synthetic idiom. In his introduction to *Dundee Doldrums* (Galliard, 1991), he describes how he came to write in Scots for the first time in 1982, when he was 21:

> At that point, I was writing in English and, although I had read MacDiarmid,
> Garioch, etc., with interest, I thought of them as a historically discrete unit,
> tied up with nationalist dogmas I didn't share. My main influence was …
> Allen Ginsberg and, more specifically, the Kerouac of *Mexico City Blues*.

Writing in response to the "deadness" of his home town, Dundee, Herbert found "the sounds, some clearly Dundonian, some more inarticulate, were apparently coming from an internal source". The English element was soon "almost wholly overwhelmed", but, "No one in my generation was producing work in Scots that I considered even vaguely interesting, and I certainly couldn't think of anyone who would want to read what I might end up producing." He solved the problem of his text's "unfinished noise" by turning to the dictionary, where he found that "the kind of words I was straining for were there… The dictionary is simply that part of the language we would have understood innately had Scots not become a subject tongue, persecuted into rural corners and forgotten." He found sufficient confidence that Scots – as seen in the "gap between Garioch's urban poetry and that of, say, Tom Leonard, and the distance I felt from the aggression in Leonard's personae" – was actually "a living tongue with its own rapidly developing literature."

The results of Herbert's experimentation are sometimes *as dense as* MacDiarmid's early lyrics but are manifestly not *derivative* from them, or from Lallans more generally. The idiom is – exuberantly – urban and contemporary. Some may find it as "aggressive," in effect, as Leonard's:

> These auld hae lost thir men and time;
> auld wummen, clochecappit, fat,
> layirs an layirs o ancient undirwear;
> sit doon, alane, ankliesswole, readin:
> Romance, Nursis' Luv, D.C. Thompson Times –
> mappamundi o a tapewurm; smell o pee,
> innards whinge wi age, blethirs quake...

Which brings us to Glasgow. If writing in Scots is going on well today, it must be because it works in the west, where the greatest concentration of Scots live, and a remarkable proportion of them respond to writing like this, from Liz Lochhead:

> Country: Scotland. Whit like is it?...
> National flower: the thistle.
> National pastime: nostalgia.
> National weather: smirr, haar, drizzle, snow.
> National bird: the crow, the corbie, le corbeau, moi!
> How me? Eh? Eh? Eh? Voice like a choked laugh. Ragbag o' a
> burd in ma black duds, a' angles and elbows and broken oxter
> feathers, black beady een in ma executioner's hood. No braw,
> but Ah think Ah ha'e a sort of black glamour.

Mary Queen of Scots Got Her Head Chopped Off, Penguin, 1989, p. 11

Lochhead (or at least her publisher) isn't bothered at all about linguistic purity – witness the intrusion of apostrophes of elision marking abbreviation into those noble Lallans words "o", "a" and "hae". Lochhead usually voices her verse in standard English. In her play, quoted above, she uses Scots because it is dramatically not just appropriate but necessary – La Corbie is chorus and voice of Scotland and serves to lead the audience back to a time when the contrast in language between Scotland and southern England was relatively clear.

Nor is Leonard a diehard user of the Glasgow phonetics which spring to mind when his name is mentioned. Much of his best verse is in standard English. But the effect of his Glaswegian utterance has been enormous. As with his junior, Herbert, there was an American influence – the non-metaphoric poetry of Carlos Williams – but the impact in Scotland has been such as to liberate voices in Muirhouse as well as Castlemilk, east as well as west, free them to make literary use of the demotic of the schemes:

> right inuff
> ma language is disgraceful
>
> ma maw tellt mi
> ma teacher tellt mi
> thi doactir tellt mi
> thi priest tellt mi...
> sum we smout thit thoat ah hudny read chomsky tellt mi
> a calvinistic communist thit thoat ah wuz revisionist tellt mi
> po-faced literati grimly kerryin thi burden a thi past tellt mi
> po-faced literati grimly kerryin thi burden a thi future tellt mi...
> even thi introduction tay thi Scottish National Dictionary tellt mi
> Ach well
> all livin language is sacred
> fuck thi lohta thim   (from 'The Ghostie Men')

Leonard jests in deadly earnest on the language issue. Like James Kelman, whose influence on prose has equalled Leonard's on younger poets, he would see formalised, institutionalised Lallans as just as oppressive as standard English. People have a right to their own speech, their own culture, which nationalist as well as internationalist grammarians, and their allies in education and the media, seek to deny them. The use by these writers of specifically Glaswegian demotic has been an example for Irvine Welsh and Duncan Maclean on the east coast – and could supply a model anywhere in the country where local speech differs markedly from standard English.

When William Alexander published *Johnnie Gibb of Gushetneuk* in 1871, carefully spelling out, to preserve it, the rural north-eastern speech of his characters, he used, as Roderick Watson notes, "formal English for passages of objective narrative and comment" and this "tends to distance him from his creation(s)..." (*The Literature of Scotland*, Macmillan, 1984, p. 288) Kelman, like Leonard, eschews such distance. Which brings me back to worry about Irvine Welsh.

Muirhouse demotic dominates large tracts of Welsh's earlier books, *Trainspotting* and *The Acid House*, where the narrative persona is often disturbingly close to characters who use language, recalling Herbert's term, "aggressively". Does the "high-low" distance opened up at once in *The Marabou Stork Nightmares* create a new version of "pastoral"? The reader may find the "spontaneous" and "naïve" use of Muirhouse speech "touching" in a way that evokes "humour" and "nostalgia" (both present in *Johnnie Gibb*). It would seem to me negative if such usage came again to be a fashionable form of "local colour", as in the Kailyard or weak "Alexandrian" Lallans. But in spite of early alarm, I feel easy that Welsh knows what he's up to. His use of a form of Scots is directly appropriate as well as "opportunistic" in a non-opprobrious sense. It works. The younger Scottish writers of merit in verse and in prose use Scots unsentimentally when – practically – it suits them to do so.

And "pastoral" is in itself a respectable mode. Burns knew how to use it. I am haunted by a remark by the late actor-playwright Roddy Macmillan: "There is nothing wrong with sentiment as long as it's *good* sentiment." (Quoted in Alasdair Cameron, ed: *Scot-Free: New Scottish Plays*, Nick Hern Books, 1990, pp. ix–x) If I have seemed to be suspicious of the use of Scots to evoke "Georgian" and "pastoral" sentiment it is because when the sentiment is not good, but false and feeble, it can be very sickly. But at best it is precisely the power of Scots words to evoke "sentiment" more freshly and sharply than English equivalents (which, anyway, don't always exist) – the power found in so many of our great songs – which gives writing in Scots a major rationale. In Sheena Blackhall's 'Keenin', a sentiment which might seem clichéd in English cuts home in Doric, because the language belongs with the landscape evoked and the speaker who also belongs:

> An fit's a larick wid?
> A widsman widna dauchle in the tellin...

Timmer, rosit, an trunk,
A quick faa, a keen aix,
A pun in the pooch, fur fellin.
Nae tae me – a wid's a hantle mair:
A green win – a reeshle i' the air,
A lane stag, bellin...

(*Hame-drauchtit*, Rainbow, 1987, p.36)

And in Tom Scott's 'The Mankind Toun', the old yearning for New Jerusalem is keen and urgent in Scots as it might not seem in standard English:

Shall we never find
The toun whaur love
Rules mankind?
Whaur the hawk, the dove,
And houlet form
A trinity
That keeps frae hairm
Ilk chimney tree?
Whaur first is laist
And ilk and ane
Gie free their best
Til brither-men?

(Dunn, ed, *Faber Book*, pp. 180–1)

The Folk Revival which Hamish Henderson hadn't launched in 1948 and which occasioned what he has recently dubbed his "muckle flyting" with MacDiarmid, who pretended to believe that folksong was intellectually worse than insignificant, (H.H., 'Zeus as Curly Snake', *Cencrastus* 52, pp 7–9) does now seem in retrospect a vitally necessary step forward for literature as well as music beyond the Grievian 'Renaissance". It helped give resonance, force and point to the literary use not of one, but of many forms of Scots, to promote the idea that any form of Scots speech could be made artistically expressive and intelligible. Since the large audience for the fiction of Kelman and Welsh seems to include at least a few of the kind of people they write about, another step forward came in the 1980s and early 1990s. So long as writers connect with the language people in Scotland actually speak, "writing in Scots" has a sound and enduring basis.

Ian McDonough

Melting Weather

Out of season, snow covered all our year,
and nothing leaving footprints
walked the streets. It was a time for fires,
counting former blessings, checking children,
damping down desires, for reading rusty entrails
of slow clocks.

But today it has arrived, the melting weather:
snowmen weep themselves to death
in every garden. Tomorrow all that lingers
will be buttons, pipes, and scarves,
half-hidden in the springing grass.

We have had enough of snowmen, whispering
cold nothings
in drowsy ears, winking at the children,
spreading icy fingers
on the treasures of the heart.

Still we wait inside, reluctant to emerge
and greet the melting weather,
guessing that, returning,
we might find doors barred, snowmen
snuggled by the fire. And us out there,
with buttons, pipes, and scarves,
rooted to the winter ground,
discovering our eyes
have smithereened to frosted glass.

Illustration by Ruth Bailey

A Lullaby of the Clan MacHine

Hush now, the glen is sleeping
Keepers are in Lodges, listening
to their treasure drinking
Ben Badh's wind is hunting
but the door is barred
This is the only world
You are the only child
The rest is dreaming

Dreaming of being with you in Glengolly

Maybe it was just being there, the light,
the time of year, the room
you coughed yourself to death in.

I had been in a land of black stars
torn down by an affair fought out in violent skies.
And now I felt your presence everywhere.

Dreaming of walking with you in Glengolly,
before Dunkirk, tuberculosis,
and the slamming doors of pain.
With waterfalls running sweetly through your veins,
your frame as weatherproof as silver birch,
the world as easy as a meadow.

I want to reach back through the glass of years,
bring you comfortable breezes,
give myself some rest.
Dreaming of being with you in Glengolly,
I woke, to find that you had calmed
a windswept hillside of my emptiness.

Crab

Needs must, spare me the squealing
Function equals beauty minus frills
Hard facts in cold pools
A sideways look, quick nip and tuck
My flesh blooms in the dark like roses

Look like a rock, feel like a rock
The tide pulls steady in my rocky heart
Lover, I wear my bones inside-out
Beware of those who hide a shell beneath their skin

John Dixon

Highland Games At Glenfinnan

The smell of seaweed at Locheil
and then the long collapse of hills
till literally is over

It's back to last year's sacking, septic tanks
and sheep-dog disinfectant. Tents that have
been pacamacked since Munich make their last
but one more re-appearance harping at
their strings like tactless clarsachs. Even if
the rain is here again then so's the Free
Church cash and carry, a policeman's van,
and someone hymning to the Hebrides...

> "...All the ways that there aren't I have furthered their air
> and returned it untouched on the stength of what's there.
> All the light that has gone, all the lengths of a day
> all I've lost to the sight of myself on their way
> and now you..."

The mist retires from some stray trees. "It might
just clear", they said so back in Corpach, more
to please the tourists than for anything.
But still there's time, it's only half past three,
although they've held the dancing and replayed
this dumb announcement on the absence
of some reprehensible Canadian:
"The one who broke a caber on Tiree".

> "...So it goes, or at least it will soon
> till there's nothing to show for this faint afternoon
> but an evening intent on the night. I could tell
> by your air that you'd never been up in it, spell-
> bound although it might be..."

> The only sounds are widowed reeds
> and dreams that never married.
> Or is it just the sea relapsing
> into silence where our sighs went?

...It was slight, almost still
as if waiting for me to remain where I will
for the rest of my life and yet all I could do
was remember to stay where you weren't, while the view
went on dying...

That said there's nothing much to do, with midge
or ice-cream from a sales van, drinks that cost
the price of their marquee, some murky
but "Romantic" cardshop and an entrance fee
to the Committee tent where "Camerons
are welcome free." You can imagine why..."
"The next event will be the men's half mile"...
A camera manufactures one more smile.

"...If half of me's you and the one
of us goes with the other then what's to be done
with those graves that were never as far from the earth
as we thought, just interring for all they were worth."

All buckled up like somebody impressed
by "The Chevalier" it can't quite place
the "Real Clan Knitwear Shop". "There didn't used
to be one". No. But then there wasn't
anything a century ago, at all,
at least of this; just plain TB and shiploads
of dilapidated people. Opening
that trap up would be pointless. Time to go.

       The smell of seaweed at Locheil
       and then the long collapse of hills
       till literally is over.

II

    With evening it's a different matter; trees
    are fading westward, shadows at their ease.
    Just what is this place doing here apart
    from trading darkness with the landscape? All
    that'll reflect itself's that waterfall
    on Braigh Umhachan flattering a start
    that's still to finish with it: Some old lengths
    of decongested grandstand, half a float,
    and swarms of an emaciated note
    about what's doing next year. Now the stength's
    gone out of them again the grass can dress
    in time for autumn. Everything gets less
    until its legendary and then just lost
    as Scotland'll discover to its cost.

III

And now, there is nowhere on earth to share
the air that was raised from our dead, just where
it ended. Another hour more or less
here, what does it matter? The cemeteries
are still out to Tara and Sleat, our breath
at rest between stars. All we learned of death
was dying; beyond that though, nothing. So
we'll leave without going one day and know
we're there by that path which'll stengthen on
our way until there is only one
place left, wherever we lie, while this,
the little we take for these skies and kiss
as if it could come back to life, just cries
all over again. Into paradise.

Songs of Exile and Return

I. Alexander Selkirk At Mas A Tierra

This block of coast, these sackcloth skies, that queue
of flannelled sunlight stirred to whitewash, what
a place to die, to live for in the mean –
time and disarm me of myself. I used
to mind, though never so it showed, just touched
my shadow slightly and was sized up by
its emptiness. So think of Strome, those hills
I lowered out among their isles, of fly –
blown Leith and Edinburgh's "style". And think
of... think of dying; anywhere. It's all
the same. My Scotland was a crime against
its punishment, and probably is still.
It's just that I can't think of her beyond
this strict comparison, just that I'm unreal.

II. Just South Of The Highlands

Kilsyth, Colzium, Callander, Dunblane,
what places do between their names, the space
they make of dreams. Or is it just a case
of me, of coming to be gone again
and gardening the night to let it seed,
while out of sight the light goes on with what
will only leave immediately. Not
that time should matter, now, it has to be

and is, that's all. If dusk collapses out
amongst the stars then so will this, from far
away to further still, till where we are
might just as well be here, this space about
to pour upon a hill. Whatever's gone
was only going off to come back on.

III. In Praise Of The Monadhliath

They're only blinds I know, a roll of empty light
amongst tomorrow, yet re-modernised as well,
so's days can dry the rain off by the night and right
the wind the wrong way up in private. Truth, to tell,
is nothing here, just what it might have felt like as
some dream drew nearer and the world went on with what
we thought was admiraton of itself in "was" –
"forever" – "afterwards" – or "one day soon", but not
somehow, in this sheer air, where everywhere is raw
with sawn-off shotgun rooms and emigrating stone
on shattered stairs. Here everything goes out alone
to get back down to earth through depths that soar, as though
the dark were curtain-calling on a landslide-show
to let its dusk down. "There, the world is at your door".

IV. Telegraph Poles In Glen Affric

This it seems all that's left of the little I owned
though not everything. Phones off the hook of my heart
I can hear them still ring from as far as the death
of my dreams, just as here in this evening apart
from itself with the past talking into its light
all my silence can wait for's a call to come through
on the night. I shall listen a little while longer
a ghost to the touch and remember to make
what I can of the sky. It will go, just as everything
does, it will go; like the pines boarded up
in those telegraph poles the line will go dead.
Yet the echo will call just as though we were whole
through these hills, and their stones, and that music which comes
within sight of itself and goes through my soul.

The Doo

William Graham

Adam was a quait, inbiggit man, keepin himsel ti himsel; and nou that his wife had slippit awa, he passed mair and mair o his time in the gairden, whyles delvin and howe-in and rakin, whyles nid-noddin and wysin awa the oors on the simmersait ablow the tree whaur she had fed the speugs and blackies and robins, and whaur they still kept flichterin doun like they expeckit her oot wi their pick onie time nou.

There was a six-fuit stane dyke atween him and his neibours on the tae side, and a heich, close-plantit beech hedge on the tither, sae he had little caa ti troke wi onie o them. He kent they thocht he was a fremmit, affstaunin character, but he let them think what they wantit, sae lang's they didna stert stickin their nebs inti his business.

Yae thing he regrettit – a daftlike thing nae dout; but aa her life hersel had been faur owre saft-skinned and skeerie-mindit for her ain guid, and wi little else adae throu the lang winter nichts, she had workit aff her parritch-hertitness devourin aa the romantic lee-buiks and trashlike novelles she could lay hauns on, richt inti her auld age. There wad hae been nae great hairm in't, gin she had juist stoppit at that; but at the hinner end, she stertit yammerin about hou nice it wad be if the twa o them gaed back yae day up the Clyde valley ti the bonnie orchard kintra whaur in their young days they had dune maist o their courtin. No in the caur aither, but in the bus up fae Glesca as they had dune in the auld days, gettin aff near the tap end o the valley and walkin back alang the river as faur's Crossfuird or Rosebank or they got the bus back hame.

He had kept pittin her aff. Clydeside wasna the place it had been when they were young. And this flea-luggit norie o hers ti tak the bus sae faur up the valley then traipse aa the road back ti Rosebank was juist owre rideeclous for words. Oniewey, what wad they look like – a couple o auld geezers wannerin haun in haun across the fields, speilin jaggy-wire fences and lowpin owre ditches and sheuchs, gettin their claes rippit and their feet clarty-wat, and quite likely their daith o cauld inti the bargain?

Still she kept craikin and craikin till, fair deived and worn doun wi't aa, he made up his mind that, come the first spell o guid wather, he wad let her hae her will o't.

But then she tuik a bad turn, and the craikin stoppit; and even when she got back on her feet and held on for a whylie langer, she never made mention o Clydeside again.

It was yae nicht at the gloamin exackly a year eftir her daith that it happent. Adam had lately been lossin aa interest in his gairden, and the place was gettin geylies ontidy and owregrown wi weeds. Aawhere owregrown excep the bed o roses he had plantit forenent the simmersait ablow the tree.

It was the backend o the year and gettin a wee thing cauld ti be sittin ootside eftir dayset. It was juist as he was about ti heize himsel up on ti his feet that he thocht he heard a soun like the flappin o wings. Like eneuch a late-on-the-go blackie eftir a forenicht pick.

Then he heard it again. Then –

"Rickietie-coo...Rickietie-coo..."

He lookit up. It was perkit on the tapmaist brainch o the tree. A bonnie snaw-white doo – lookin back doun at him and yirkin its heid back and forrit, like it was tryin ti gar him tak tent.

He kent it was rideeclous. It was juist that he wantit to think it was hersel come back ti tell him he was forgien.

The orra body

Ay, yon's him aa richt – the huddery wee craitur across the street wi the secfu o guid-kens-what owre his shouther, and the aye-bydan lug-ti-lug grin on his face. That'll be him awa up ti his ludgins in the graveyaird howff wi his latest uptak o pig-brock ootwales fae the butcher's and baker's or they shut up shop for the weekend. Syne he'll be layin intil't wi aa the gust o a dukemalordie conisoor.

As ye micht expeck, Neddy's a naitral for aa the toun's smert alecs. Yin o their maist gallus characters is the toun sculptor's prentice-haun, Davie Freeman. Davie fand Neddie in the graveyaird yae day whaur, in return for bein allooed to nicht in the howff, he whyles helpit Andra Duffy, the cemetery owresman, at the grave-diggin.

Davie was snoddin up a heidstane no faur fae whaur Neddy and Andra were howkin oot the last restin-place o a wife whase man had dee't twa-three month aforesyne, and a braw new tombstane had aareadies been ereckit at the grave-heid. Eftir a wee, Andre gaed alang ti the howff for a mornin cup o tea, and left Neddy ti cairry on wi the wark.

Eftir the owresman was weill oot o sicht, young Davie creepit up ahin the new tombstane. Aa o a sudden the wee man, diggin faurer and faurer inti the grun, heard a palsifyin groan. Then an oorie, graveyaird vyce thirled in his lugs –

"Caa canny, Neddy. Caa canny..."

Struck stane-still, Neddy glowered at the grun ablow his feet. Then wi a stamagastit screich he bunged his spade aside, sprauchlt up oot the grave, and gaed teirin doun ti the cemetery gate like the hunds o Hell were gurlin at his heels.

Andra Duffy sweirs he never saw hunt or hare o the wee man in, or oniewhere near, the graveyaird for a twalmonth eftirwairds.

Then there was the time that Sam Kirby, the hearse and taxi hirer, was hosin doun yin o his caurs in the yaird at the faur end o the toun fae the cemetery. It was a bitter-cauld winter mornin, wi a snell wind skirlin alang the high street. Sam hadna the caumest o tempers at the best o times. He had juist had a tiff wi his wife in the yaird office, and what wi that and a getherin heid cauld and a wind like ti freeze the end-on dreip at his nose, he was juist in the tid ti gie the first body that crossed his path the ful brunt o his ill-temper.

Neddy was that body. It wasna the first time he had slippit inti the office, wi Sam's wife's permission, for a heat at the fire. And it wasna the first time that Sam had tellt him ti tak his hotchin, flea-bitten corp aff the premises or he ran him oot the door – and warnt his wife what wad happen ti her gin she ever alloued the wee messan back owre the doorstane again. Sae this parteeclar mornin, when he cotch Neddy slinkin back in, he fairly let flee.

Flingin his still-rinnin hose ti the grun, he beltit across the yaird and inti the office. There, shair eneuch, was the wee scrog haudin up the back-flaps o his jaiket, and birslin his backside forenent the bleizin fire.

Dancin mad, Sam linkit across the flairheid, cleikit Neddy by the scriff o the neck, and breingen him back oot inti the yaird. Then, grabbin the hose aff the grun, he turnt it ful blast on Neddy and raired –

"Gin we canna kill 'em, we'll droun 'em!"

Sowpin-wat rags clingin ti the rickle o banes that was his body, Neddy gaed skelpin oot the yaird and alang the street. He feenisht up whumperin and keenin at the kirk manse door. The minister's wife tuik him in and fittit him oot wi a dry semmit and shurt, and a jaiket and trousers, wi a het cup o tea inti the bargain.

That did Sam Kirby and his caur-hirin business nae guid, I can tell ye. But as for Neddy, the hale toun felt a warm gleesh o kindness for him and the minister's wife. And when that had feenally brunt itsel oot, the wee man developed a bad cauld and a rackin cough ti gang wi't; and what wi that and the new ootfit o minister's claes he had gotten himsel, he had never felt crouser or mair weill-dune-ti in aa his born days.

David Summers

Variations on a Theme from THE MAGIC FLUTE

I

A polygonal chamber of mesh and fret
stands there, in my childhood, damp structure
of dark green painted wood against which
glowed the plumage of that bird...

its colour like a concatenated burst,
what colour could be, colour in earnest,
a living spectrum of colour, juxtaposed
against a world drained, devoid, insipid.

in imagination the startling radical cry,
flashing, fluttering arc of that trajectory,
plummage like a flare bursting in my head,
bright direction in a darkening canopy.

II

The compulsion to meaning,
compacting all colour to a point,
all history to a single thread,
all life, a concentrated act:
one claw hooked into the mesh,
the hard beak clouts the wood.

This compression belongs to me,
a shapeless fusion into memory
staring at me until blood runs cold,
the bird abruptly speaks my word
back to me, meaning obscured,
message detached, absurd.

So what replaces intellect
is modulation of the throat,
is the piercing repetition of a note:
Talk! Tawk! Ta-awk! it shrieks out,
followed by the uncomfortable pause
before it cracks a nut.

III

An old question of rote,
meaning abandoning word
by the act of having it said,
the act of repeating the note
until the melodic line is set
in an upward spiralling loop,
a whirling chorusing troupe
sweeping across the skies,
silk that is blue and red
and billowing like flags
or green and white instead,
evanescent trailing scripts,
how ideas take sudden flight
like illuminating threads
drawn up into the light...

Yet words *per se* are dead:
husks and broken shells
crumble from the perch
to the floor of grit and dirt,
black-and-white deposit
that hardens where it falls,
the crap, the slop, the shit,
the residue of spirit...

IV

The reality we hold,
the reality we hear,
cackled tactile fear:
beak cocks and skews,
talons grip the wire,
clatter as they climb,
all hammering tongs,
hard hook of the beak
clambers and clangs,
strikes violently, shrieks,
belies the soft blend
of iridescent calm,
the saturating smear
of colour on the plate,
blue with violet glimmer,
a scarlet after-image
embedded into green,
blue penetrates yellow,
the soft receptive hue,
the reality we see,
the reality we dream...

V

– A metallic green shading into blue?
shading into yellow? a blush of red?
creation must have wings to spread,
be accomplished and articulate too,

must be able to claw his own way up
whatever barricades have been erected,
must fight for attention, fight for respect,
be able to drill home his argument

into the diffident affections of a mate,
then reproduce and reproduce with gusto...
But all this perfection that we create
may seem in the event oh so ungrateful,

perfection can seem hunted and cheated
with an awkward, persistent gift of recall,
and a shrill voice uncannily like our own
mocking our exorbitant capacity for detail...

VI

That somehow colour
can be captured by us,
enmeshed as it were
in our designs,
Graeco-Roman letters
in coded permutation,
RUFUS gives a clue
of crimson in the flame,
pumping the gas lamp
until the GALBINUM
casts smudged shadows
into the shrinking room,
– that piston squeak –
the twin mantle bursts
into brilliant WHITE
in a globe, encompassing...

The captive light
remains alive
long in the memory,
a transformation
from alphabetic
configurations of what
is essentially abstract
and without colour,
without intrinsic life

or fire of its own,
but an inert matrix
of invisible wire
which, when we breathe
upon it, we transform
into a net of words,
into song...

So imagine the bird
invisible in us
at first,
perched in us
in a vast black vault
we call the mind...
coming face to face
it begins to emerge,
green falls into place,
the ermine touch,
yellow, blue, white
falling into place,
there he is, as always:
our radiant slave
waits upon our word...
it is the miracle
of language.

VII

He lead me to a garden where many a flower grew
and as he spake to me I noted their profusion,
honeysuckle wrapping its sinuous arms around
the solid-limbed wisteria gripping the pergola,
sweet pea and sweet william tussling together
in a bed of straw, the flexing lily's buttery breath,
its captive drop of dew, flagrant tongue and flange
of iris stained in blue, peony's satin skin on
violet's velvet cushion, lilac's orb and septre,
acerbic orange and yellow of nasturtium,
tulip cups collide with bristling whisks of lavender,
the tossing globular shag-mops of the aster,
purple waxy ampules of the fuchsia, scarlet sylvia,
all this I remember... Then the knuckle and the claw

and the confusion after...

VIII

The inflexion point in life
    half expecting the worst
shifts sideways on a bench
    all scruff and callus fist,
feathers blustered into fluff
    with a bleary look of pastiche,
a resigned cock of the wig,
    "I was not always like this."

How life begins to decay,
    sheen turns into drab,
what once seemed fresh and free
    becomes this narrow cage
of farce and borrowed phrase,
    how age would parody youth
if legs would only obey,
    "It was not always thus."

Pleasure spits in our face,
    the public changes its taste,
how values we used to esteem
    seem vacuous and inane
or ambitious and out-of-place,
    if only we could do it again
we'd live the life of our dreams,
    if only we had perceived

the emptiness that awaits.

IX

That

smoke smudged red in milky light
of stained-glass cathedral overhead,
incense vaporizing into the vault
as celibate cleric in brocaded silk
(where gold and emerald interlock)
unblemished by sordid stain of lust
yet in youthful vigour of his health
and firm supplication of his mouth,
his gabbled voice, muscular enough,
rises like a bird, invisible, remote...

That

old transvestite, fetching in a skirt,
green lamé hitched above the knee
(fluffy sulphurous *boa* about the neck)
perched on a stool, but precariously,
one elbow anchored securely to the bar,
she holds a cigarette and slowly blows
smoke into the fetid air, lips' red
rich succulence of sexuality,
she swivels her legs for all to behold,
lets out a shriek of laughter there...

                    That

puffed-up figure of Authority
shrieking for attention on the bridge,
satin ribbons strewn on his lapel,
insignia and braided epaulets...
An officer knows what truth to tell,
knows the meaning of 'distensible'...
Don't be a fool. Play the game.
He nods; he winks; he knowing-looks;
he opens wide his maw to reveal
tongue like a dildo, brain like a bean.

                    That

piece of kitsch, bald, half-finished,
supine upon a taxidermist's bench,
skin stretched taut onto wire mesh,
(mirror, vessel, burgeoning alter-ego)
this soft tissue he manipulates,
makes of blankness opaque material,
gives to silence his own context,
with his deft touch, transfixes life
lest it stand apart, lest it turn-tail,
lest before cock shriek, it deny us.

                    That Glove.

                    X

          Intellect transforms
          translucent Word,
          that solid silicon
          to colour and song.

              Look in the crystal:
              light subdivides into
              unique spectral lines,
              a life in its detail...

          Solidity transformed,
          sublimating iodine,
          an indigo feather
          floats in the mind.

Issy McKnight

Memorabilia

Two plants
Like fat frolicking spiders
Now flourish happily
In your boots

Stoked

Your sky today
Crimson burst at tea
Encircling mashed potato clouds.
Cloissonné
Fixing river pink
From that silver grey
Tinting swans to Battenburg
Hills to midnight blue
Transporting back to other lives
Apricots with scarlet hue.

Doors

All that hesitation
Then encouraged by your presence
Beyond those scary doors
I entered – free searching.

On that side
A waterfall
Dislodging all inhibitors
Ghosts gone and debris dumped

Out there and on it
We flew high and far beyond Kendal Mint
Where Venus and Pluto fuse
In oneness with universe.

Paths

He took me to B&Q
Asda's and Videoshack
As s treat on Saturdays

You took me to my I.Q .
New paths and Kaleidoscope land
As a daily matter of rightness

I now go to life
Perhaps Nirvana.

Catriona Newman

Afterthoughts

He sat on a stone
in a field.
Beneath the stone
a worm lay crushed,
beneath the worm
a stunted seed;
from inside the earth
a small life cried
within a broken stem.
In a field
on a stone,
he thought
he was the only one.

The Vigil

Deftly spun, white wool cocoons
his soul to blankets. The tiny lungs
wax and wane under a brooding eye.
Prowling the dark she tiptoes
on carpet, the same pattern of dread.
The monitor clicks,
but she's not trusting
        any tick tock machine.

Ghosting velvet, she panthers
down all of his sleepways.
Watchful round the hours.
Diligent, that each breath
should burst into another.
        Nightly, with a haunted heart,

she crouches outside the slatted gloom,
        plucking at the sleeve of God.

The Shore Walkers

November morning, salted after the storm.
Early out walking, our heels sinking
into wet galaxies of sand,
star strewn.
Yes, and we as time travellers
finding sudden treasure at our feet!
Mad storm dragon came down under dark,
foraging wildly among waves,
his tail a-lashing spiked dragnet
raking up the deep.
Now, fluted and fantastic,
spaceships crashed onto the beach.

Giant mussel shells too,
flashing rainbows in my palm.
Un-numbered ocean children,
from a night of thunder and war.
Orphaned at my shorebound feet
with doors agape, I could
peer into these,
worlds within worlds, as any
curiously passing,

                    Keyhole Kate.

In Conclusion

A shrug, a suck, old man's teeth slipping.
Rain splashed over-shoulder words,
aimed across the Tuesday air, and missing
the windy bus-stop crowd.

Words meant for anyone-for-no-one-for-God,
spoken down eons, trumpeting blow.
Grubby wings fly the lost prayers.
Random philosophies, where do they go
but along gutters and over rooftops?

Old one, unloved, from the bitten north,
finds ears in a queue with time to sell,
looked down at the contents of his soul, then
resigned and in conclusion chose to tell
a summing-up of everything,

with: "Late agen. What a life, ye ken."

Reviews

Crossing Borders

A History Maker, Alasdair Gray, Canongate, £13.99;
Feersum Endjinn, Iain M Banks, Orion, £15.99;
Something Very Like Murder, Frank Kuppner, Polygon, £9.95

Alasdair Gray's latest novel is a characteristically frolicksome *jeu des lettres* – part science fiction satire, part sermon; like an Escher drawing somehow less than, and yet more than a novel.

The story itself is frankly a bit thin. Set some time after the End Of History, it concerns 'Superbly muscled' Wat Dryhope, lieutenant to Craig Douglas, commander of the Ettrick clan, and hero of the last stand that causes all the trouble. This is a world where sport and politics, and competitive pursuits generally, are fought out in Sealed Knot manner with real swords and guns. The military inclinations of the human race are satisfied by organised battles in which life, limb and honour is at stake, but not land, religion or ideology. Among the Northumbrian clans ranged against the Ettricks are the Milburns and the Charltons, as if to emphasise the boys' game element in this stylised warfare. (For the uninitiated, these are the names of famous 20th century Northumbrian footballers.)

The Ettricks face ultimate defeat, having so far manipulated the Geneva Convention's rules to avoid yielding their standard. Douglas comes up with a scheme that again snatches a face-saver from the jaws of defeat. It isn't a victory – not with the clan troops virtually exterminated – but it is, under Convention rules, a draw. So brilliantly conceived a draw is it that the entire world pays attention. Wat becomes a celebrity in its wake, with the consequence that the Clan appoints him commander-in-chief, while he also attracts the seductive attentions of Delilah Puddock. Order is threatened, but ultimately restored, and history continues to be over.

Gray cites as stimulus for this book criticism by Alan Bold that his work is insufficiently Scottish. In consequence, *A History Maker* is thick with jokes both erudite and demotic, largely at the expense of Bold's point of view. There is deep and widely-read scholarship behind the Borders clan system Gray describes, modelled largely on Hogg and Scott. The business of the brilliant draw is preceded by a passage lifted – with spin of Gray's own making – from Hogg's *Three Perils of Man*, where the Northumbrian, faced with the execution of his brother, chooses to fight on rather than concede to the enemy, even though reason dictates the latter course.

Where Hogg's Scots is natural, Gray's is deliberately artificial. His choice of Scots words tends either to colour from time to time with the odd wouldnae, or ramfeezle with comical-sounding drollerie. Gangrel rather than caird, for example, is the kind of choice Gray makes. He is deliberately overstating the superficiality of this kind of place-names and Scots-words approach to Scottish identity in order to debate it. After all, if you changed the words to those of another language, if you changed the location to, say, the Welsh borders, would this still be a Scottish novel? It's an improbable task, but the answer must be yes, since the whole thing is suffused with an attitude to community that is distinctively Scottish. If you were going to try and pin it down to a place, the Marxist subtext, each according to their needs etc, is more readily associated with Glasgow than Birmingham, and certainly more so than Moscow. The significant, skilfully-handled, role of women in the society he describes is characteristic of the old pre-Clearance rural Scotland (while other patterns of this imagined society also recall stable aboriginal cultures, such as the Maori).

As a satire, then, on male traits such as competitiveness *A History Maker* can be counted a success. Whether it can be regarded as a blueprint for a tenable *modus vivendi* is less certain. A more hardnosed analysis would no doubt tell us whether the copy of *Ten Days that Shook the World* that Wat obtains was the edition with the introduction by Lenin and references to Trotsky removed (as published by the CPGB after John Reed's death) or not. In a more hardnosed analysis, that would be relevant. Nevertheless, as that remark proves, Gray has an extraordinary talent for provoking thought and discussion with, on the face of it, the slightest of means.

Are the writings of Iain M. Banks sufficiently Scottish? Alan Bold is probably an exception in doubting Alasdair Gray's Scottish credentials, but no one seems to ask this of more commercial writers such as Banks. I hesitate to use the term 'commercial', since *Lanark* surely qualifies Gray as a 'commercial' author. Indeed, how does the literary world know instinctively when to turn its nose up? Arguably, the same Scottish sense of community suffuses *Feersum Endjinn*, as it does in other Banks novels, with the M and without. It has been said of Science Fiction that it frees authors from certain constraints implicit in the conventional novel, particularly in dealing with society's conventions. I don't buy that. Both Doctor Who and Star Trek, to take two of the most familiar SciFi phenomena, retain a strong link both with Earth and with points of view concerning morality entirely dependent on the dominant ideology of the respective countries of origin. Just as Gray's future world is of a Scottish imagination, so too is Banks'.

It's worth saying that the story-telling skill *Feersum Endjinn* shows is exemplary. The narrative technique has a contemporary familiarity, following the plot from the democratically-rotated viewpoints of each character in turn. As soon as one point of view ends, you feel irritated that it has been cut off *just there*, but sense that you are getting the same feeling of irritation every time this happens.

The plot is difficult to summarise, but concerns an assumed contract of trust between ruler and ruled that is in danger of being breached. The interest of the community is being threatened by the élite's pursuit of its own interest. The Crypt, a kind of collective consciousness, retains experience and knowledge of issues that show the élite's actions to be dangerous and short-sighted. Access to the Crypt is hazardous, and requires the special talents of a few psychically gifted individuals, Tellers, such as the novel's hero Bascule. Bascule's interaction with the Crypt begins with his encounter with Ergates the mechanical ant, and his role in bringing about the denouement is prompted throughout by Ergates or the absence of Ergates. Remarkably, Banks is able to make you care about a mechanical ant, and I mean really *care*. Further, the language of Bascule's narrative differs from the rest in such a way that you have no option but to take more care reading it:

> Coarse its all a bit murki & weerd down thare in thi kript & moast bags (thas Boys & Girls remembir) get a bit spooked even thinkin about contactin thi ded let alone actuly welcomin them in2 ther heds & ½in a natter wif them. 2 us tellirs tho iss juss sumthin we do as a mattir ov coarse & no bothir ... well, providin u r carefil, naturily (admitidly ther arnt a lot ov old tellirs aroun, tho thas moastly coz ov what they col naturil wastidje).

Does that remind you of *Back in the Jug Agane* or does it remind you of Tom Leonard? There's a bit of both in there. The effect is to foreground Bascule's narrative – indeed it proves to be the most important as the community asserts itself over the élite and the contract between ruler and ruled is re-established. Like Alasdair Gray, Banks presents a frivolous surface at first glance far distant from contemporary life. But like Gray, that frivolous surface invites a close look beneath.

Something Very Like Murder is very unlike the other two books: instead of a hyper-imaginary world, Frank Kuppner's is hyper-real. Suspiciously real. The core of the narrative concern's the death of the author's mother, and subsequently his father too. Kuppner starts out with reflections, presented as pages of a journal, on coincidence, synchronicity, and murder, beginning with research conducted for his previous *A Very Quiet Street*.

The central strand relates the murder, by one Bertie Willox, of his father in November 1929 at their home in Grove Street, Glasgow (mother/wife having died at the beginning of the year) to a web of totally unrelated murders that builds up a matrix of unexpectedness against a backdrop, related in exaggeratedly painstaking detail of the writer's own totally normal, humdrum life. It's a difficulty about the book, that humdrum detail, but a worthwhile one, since the denouement stands out shocking and stark against it. There is in any case a leavening of Kuppner's characteristically wry humour. Laughter, after all, is often our only defence against the painful, the shocking, the brutal or the grisly. The groping search for meaning in this matrix of the unforseen is movingly accomplished. Ah, but is it sufficiently Scottish? *Peter Cudmore*

Landscapes of the Imagination

Medusa Dozen, Tessa Ransford, Ramsay Head Press, £6.50; *Having Been In The City*, Alison Prince, Taranis Books, £5.99; *Landscape With Figures*, Anne Beresford, Agenda Editions, £6; *A Keen New Air*, Raymond Vettese, Saltire New Poetry, £6.99; *News of the World*, Maurice Lindsay, Scottish Cultural Press, £4.95

Medusa Dozen and other poems is Tessa Ransford's eighth collection of poems. As with her previous books it is one to mull over, to read inwardly. She combines considerable technical accomplishment with insight, wisdom and intuition to create poems brimming with ideas and arresting juxtapositions. The Medusa sequence comprises the first of four sections. In these poems she explores the two worlds inhabited by men and women, as in 'Medusa Two': "We breathe in a different element/ and make each other gasp." Each poem focuses on an intersection of these worlds, exploring power, communication and relationships. 'Medusa Four' eloquently defines love and its delusions, gently chiding the vulnerable lover who holds back from experiencing love in its fullness: "Is it too late for you to once admit/ to feelings that enhance you by their strength?/ Your dignity in hoarding them is less." There are equally strong poems in this section on the maturing influence of motherhood ('Six'), the intellectual castration of women ('Seven'), and their creative power ('Eleven'). The last poem, 'Medusa Thirteen', is an exhortation to women to choose their intuitive selves rather than their shadows: "Choose me as light:/ your shadow will fall into place."

Many of the poems draw on images from the classical world, or experiences of other cultures, particularly Japan and India. Each has something contemporary to say, to remind us of what is important: relationships, history, language. Always there is sensitivity to other ways of life, other cultures and languages. The poem 'Viewpoint' powerfully reminds us of the descriptive beauty of Gaelic names and the divide of language.

'Golden Images' is quintessential Ransford. In it she compares the grave-goods such as masks that have been plundered for archaeological enquiry or profit with those treasures of memory which are "gleamingly attached/ to the actual person, to the ones I love,/ whether they are living yet or dead." As if this were not enough for one poem, there are other associations that span ancient Egypt to the nuclear bomb. In even a short poem like 'The Clarsach' there is room for the reader's imagination. It is a poem about beauty, purpose, perfection, existence, the liveliness of the eccentric. Read too her poems set in the Scottish Borders: they are strongly rooted in the natural history of that area with a real sense of belonging.

My favourite part of the book, however, is 'Transverberation', a sequence of seven sonnets. They are poems about interdependence: poems of a gentle, restrained, mature passion. They are rhythmic and unobtrusively formal, giving the feeling of simplicity and lightness. Each successive last line is in turn the opening line of the next sonnet, like a series of musical motifs picked up and developed in new directions. The final sextet reiterates lines from the earlier sonnets, ending in a splendid crescendo in praise of poetry and love.

Having Been in the City is Alison Prince's first collection of poems, although she is well-known as an author in other fields, particularly children's books. She writes in a lucid, accessible style. Many of her poems display considerable deftness in construction: she uses form to best advantage, lightly and unpretentiously. These are immensely readable poems, covering a range of themes, all with sensitivity. Always she brings the reader to the heart of the experience. She is equally adept at writing about nature, man's dominance of nature, death and pain and our attitudes to the darker aspects of the human condition. 'Fiddle Music' for example is a simple but shocking reminder of Chernobyl.

The poems reach out to understand other people, other cultures or communities: 'Being Afraid' is a fine sonnet which explores the fear that creates barriers between black and white people. One enduring theme is home-coming, and the power of the horizon to give identity and restore inner peace, as in 'Inter City' "That sweet straight line/ Defines the limit of my being." She writes about beaches and moons too, but still finds something fresh and memorable to say. In 'New Moon in

Africa': "After the dark time, there she lies,/ Nail-paring thin." The book ends on a humorous note: the poem 'Absent-mindedness' all the more humorous for its formal structure and metrical quality. She lists the "sudden sleepings" in her head, then comments, "My absent mind is filled with the delight/ Of sweet horizons and the heron's flight."

Landscape with Figures bears the hallmarks of previous Beresford collections, in its themes – such as relationships and loss – and in the biblical allusions. She captures the dilemmas and mysteries of our humanness in poems such as 'Relic', 'Winter Sunday', and Mothers, Daughters, Mothers'. I particularly enjoyed her Monastic Interlude sequence: the language and pace of these of twelve poems is suitably sonorous, and the monastic silence simply invoked in poems like 'Kitchen'.

I found the poems with biblical allusions the most satisfying, reminiscent of earlier work in *The Curving Shore* and *The Sele of the Morning*. However, most poems had something to give pleasure, or to encourage further study: in 'Psalm', for example, or the mystical 'Walking in Twilight' ("The cold climbing from our feet/ driving our very being/ upwards and out/ towards the first star.")

A Keen New Air is Raymond Vettese's second collection of poems, his first having won the Saltire Society's First Book Award. It contains 59 poems divided into four sections: Innocence, Twa Earths, Fowk, and Ominous Engines. All poems are in a living Scots, that George Bruce in his foreword describes as "commending its warmth, wit and good humour." There is a fairly comprehensive glossary at the back of the book.

Poems which kindle memories of youth are particularly strong: the cruelty of little boys, injustice at school, the tedium of formal religion. In the first poem, with a vitality and gritty honesty typical of the collection, Vettese captures the relief of the child being let out of Sunday School: "It wis feenisht, feenisht,/ an' we were free an' dancin on the green/ wi bricht Hosannah tae the livin sun/ an the gowden-beaked gulls in the bonnie blue sky/ soonded like trumpets on Jericho's plain!"

In his love poems such as 'In Spite o White Linen' Vettese displays the sensuality and tenderness of the Scots tongue. Elsewhere,

life, death and nationalism are common threads, sometimes dealt with seriously, sometimes humorously. The book contains many poems about particular 'fowk', often outsiders or characters. Each he treats with an affectionate honesty. In the poems about his grandparents their strength of character comes through irrespective of their Scottish, Irish or Italian origin. He eloquently voices the ambivalent feelings of many first- and second-generation Italian Scots caught up in the Second World War. In 'Broken', he says of his Brechin grandfather "He gaed til Pitlochry, interned at echty/ and him in the City God kens hoo lang/ and his sons playin waltzes at the local dances."

'Shibboleth' must be one of the most serious yet light-hearted poems written about the Scots tongue. Earwigs are horniegolochs despite the teacher's insistence to the contrary, and they, like the Scots tongue, "wad survive a holocaust". There is little seeking after form. Rather the power of the poems is in the sound of the language. As he says in 'Simple Music': "I let words rant an' jig but aye/ haud them in final order thegither,/ pairtners in glee…"

Subtitled Last Poems, *News of the World* is the third and probably the last collected poems from Maurice Lindsay, a man of letters. In the title sequence he is as much moralist and journalist as poet: a John Pilger of poetry. He rebukes religious bigots and the self-righteous, decimates cult leaders, and is none too kind to muggers, murderers, warmongers, politicians, joy-riders and yuppies. His technical skill is consummate, and this lends a gravitas to the poems as "public sonnets". Of the sixteen I found 'Hospital Waiting-Room' the most striking as it has immediacy and lacks the camera-lens feeling of the others.

There is a pessimism which hangs over much of the book, for example in 'Our Times: A Coda'. But just in case anyone should carp at this balance, in a humorous sonnet 'Front Page Cartoon', he destroys his stalwart Mrs Folliat-Cholmondeley, a seeker after good news. The poems I most enjoyed were those about the end of life, 'Directions for a Funeral' and 'A Humanist Faxes Death' – moving poems, written with honesty and spirit.

Christine de Luca

Whispers in the Gallery

Morning Star Folios: Fifth Series, 5/1–5/4, Alec Finlay, 17 Gladstone Terrace (ground floor), Edinburgh EH9 1LS

"A correspondence is poetry enlarged", runs the Morning Star motto taken from Robert Duncan, and these correspondences between poets and artists, guided by the hand and mind of Alec Finlay, are delicate art objects that enlarge our understanding of what poetry is, not to mention questioning the fast-turnover hype it/pulp it approach of the pile 'em high booksellers. These are highly collectable fine art productions issued quarterly at an accessible price, available either individually at a cost of £6, or by a subscription of £20 per series.

The fifth series begins with Michael Longley's *Birds and Flowers* (5/1), seven poems on a reverse-printed folding triptych of fine paper containing a watermark of a ghost-orchid drawn by Gary Hincks. This subtlety is typical of Finlay's artistry, the understatement, the sense of there being more hidden within than is firstly apparent, and Longley's poems ('The Beech Tree', 'Sandpiper', 'Form', 'The Ghost Orchid', 'Whimbrel', 'Couplets', 'Water-lily') blend beautifully with the format, a poetry of inference, of time-stopping wonder at nature micro and macro.

5/2 is PALABAR*mas*, a correspondence between the Chilean poet Cecilia Vicuña and Edwin Morgan in two parts: the first is the actual hand-sewn folio of Vicuña's concrete word-constructions in Spanish with Morgan's Scots translations, where words are chopped into syllables to point up etymological links and chance orthographic association, such as

ver dad   **oan** esty

dad ver   **stey** oan

The second part, a stapled booklet, contains the key: 'verdad' is 'truth', while 'dad' means 'give' and 'ver' means 'insight'. Together with this glossary, a letter from Vicuña to Finlay explains her view of language: "Words are playing with me all the time... each word/ contained other words... Laughing I wrote them down, calling them riddles, because they were a question and an answer at once." Once again, this folio contains much pleasure for the reader, a delight in the hidden, partially revealed, as with the 'ghost orchid'.

Folio 5/3 is *A Language I Do Not Know*, poems translated from Estonian by Jaan Kaplinski and illustrated by Edda Renouf. At first glance, this is a straightforward combination of word and image. Kaplinski's poems are orthodox in their form, narrative-based, while Renouf's black-printed leaves seem an obvious accompaniment to the "Poplar's character/ Birches destiny, Lime's personality". But then one's eyes fix on the little stars that peep through the heart of certain of the leaves, and read again that line "the nameless star/ that glitters through its twigs". Are the constellations named in the poem there in the leaf patterns, present but unstated, a unity of the earthbound with the cosmic?

5/4 is *Morning and Evening*, a correspondence between Sam Hamill and David Connearn: white card folding into four squares, containing two translations by Hamill from the Japanese of Mibu no Tadamine (c. 920 AD) and Otomo Kuronushi (c. 8th century), and two complementary square-shaped prints by Connearn of a rippled surface, one black, the other the gentlest off-white. Here the reviewer is aided by a note from Finlay to the effect that both are rigorous students of Zen, although they have never met, and that Finlay himself set up the process whereby each made a work at dawn and dusk, separated from one another by the breadth of the Atlantic. So the presence of Finlay as artist is not immediately evident but immanent in the final artwork, his aim being "to prevent art simply illustrating poetry, or words only giving story to the image." Instead, parts sit together, integral in themselves, but each informing, relating the whole.

Because of the care necessary in handling these folios, the reader doesn't simply read but enters into a new kind of relationship with text and image – a heightened awareness of the craft behind printing- and presentation. The process of unwrapping, reading and discerning meaning is slowed down to the point of stillness. Although slight in themselves, the folios contain much invisible space between their printed areas which the reader must traverse to reach understanding. Ideas, like skeletal structures, are often hidden: this enigmatic quality gives much pleasure, and can't but inspire respect for the intelligence of their subtle, far-seeing creator.   *Robert Alan Jamieson*

A World of Difference

In the Blood, Stewart Conn, Bloodaxe, £6.95; *Western Swing*, Andrew Greig, Bloodaxe, £7.95; *Monsoon History*, Shirley Geok-lin Lim, Skoob Pacifica, £6.99; *Eucalyptus: Selected Poems 1978-1994*, Menna Elfyn, Gomer, £5.50.

Stewart Conn has been producing his own style of precisely-cadenced verse for almost thirty years now. *In the Blood* is his ninth collection, divided into three sections. Section I marks a return to Ayrshire, the county of his childhood; Section II contains poems mainly set in Edinburgh, where he now lives; and section III is a catch-all, often dealing with figures such as Boudin, John Muir, Jung and Freud.

Conn is an engaging poet and a fine craftsman. He rarely publishes a poor poem, and his tone is characterised by a careful, yet curiously thrawn, deliberation. If he seldom uses end-rhyme or regular metre one feels that this is mainly a studied avoidance, not an inability, for the poems are full of conscious, if deft, craft. The persona his poems present to the reader is a concerned and very responsible one, though not without irony, humour, and a sometimes self-implicating self-awareness. The danger of too much expressed concern for the state of the world, of course, is dullness. The poet is usually acute enough to avoid this, though occasionally poems become bogged down by their moral commentary, and one longs for the engines of that gaiety Yeats knew to come to the poet's aid. At other times, sheer documentary authenticity carries a poem.

This is true of a number of the Ayrshire pieces. They are interesting and satisfying to read by virtue of their precise craft and factual content. Socially acute and subtle, the poems do justice to, and yet mainly transcend, their geographical location, contain a good deal of contemporary and historical Ayrshire, and speak convincingly of Conn's own childhood seen from the perspective of the mature man. The book's fine first poem, 'Kilmarnock Edition', is a hilarious evocation of the young Conn as Burnsian reciter, an account prompted by the poet's wife, Judy, discovering an annotated copy of 'To a Mouse', from Conn's schooldays, complete with:

...directions to accompany that mid-50s rendering: 'Start softly': *Wee sleekit, cowrin' timorous beastie...*

'Hand on chest': *Oh what a panic's in thy breastie!* Then 'pensively': *I'm truly sorry man's dominion...* The audience mesmerised no doubt, as I mimed the *cruel coulter*, gave the *daimen icker* laldie.

From which the poet draws out the need to restate Burns' "criterion of goodness."

Section II also begins strongly, with 'Jawbone Walk', which consists of the dialogue of a tramp cadging money from passers-by, interposed skilfully with his holding forth on how where he sat was once undersea. Conn is particularly good at capturing speech patterns. Section II finishes with an attractive sequence, 'Above the Storm', written to and for the poet's wife while she is in New Zealand. The verse counterpoints domestic detail, and visits by the poet to his ailing mother, with meditations on transience, like extracts from inspired diary entries, quickened and enriched by Conn's exact language.

There is a most attractive genuineness about the best of Conn's poems. When they fail for me, they do so by his tendency to overemphasise a moral message, or occasionally through excess of detail: for example, a piece such as 'Three Ages of Man' partly breaks up under the weight of information Conn crams into it. Also, one wishes the poet would speak on occasion with fewer qualifications: trust the energy of poetry in himself more, without straining it quite so rigorously through the sieve of what it is permissible to say. Yet, too, it is perhaps energy and conscience in appropriate tension which give his successes their gravitas and power. This is a considerable collection, with a substantial number of good poems, and some that are excellent. 'Inheritance', about urban violence, is a truly modern poem. In three quatrains 'Castles' elucidates the history of four Ayrshire castles and their inhabitants. Here, Conn trusts his images. The poem concludes, with a radiant simplicity, and the beautiful jaunty-wistful cadence in the last two lines:

Colourful still, their forays;
names given to school houses –
Loudoun, Dundonald, Craigie, Dean:
red, blue, yellow, green.

Andrew Greig is also quite capable of writing excellent verse. A poem of his such as 'The Maid and I' (though he altered, bafflingly, the wonderful last line for the version published in the *Faber* Anthology), has stayed in my mind since I first read it. *The Order of the Day*, his last book, contained striking and unusual poems. I found *Western Swing* disappointing. It is a long, fragmented piece in which various characters correspond to different parts of the sensibility, and indulge in a lot of philosophical blether. If its aim was to reproduce something of the randomness of experience, it succeeds. However, there are also a number of arresting sections – interestingly, mainly when death appears, like a knock at the door late at night: the sequence opens strongly with the narrator's *timor mortis*; the section 'Tourists and Terrorists', in which the narrator and friends come face to face with extinction in the form of terrorists in the high Atlas, is compelling:

> It's that simple: sun overhead,
> four blades, the oddly plastic
> barrel of a semi-automatic
> stroked idly against the ribs.

The mix of registers in the poem is refreshing, it contains vigour, and humour, but not enough of it is memorably expressed. It is perhaps no coincidence that of those Greig thanks in his acknowledgements (as well as Norman MacCaig with his *Glenmorangie*), two are academics. Some academics may well have a vested interest in complex – or long-winded – texts. *Western Swing* is a perfect vehicle for annotation, discussion, and thesis-writing. Greig's notes at the end of the book parody those of 'The Waste Land'. He 'samples' – lifts, from many sources – parts of other texts. But I don't know how many common readers (like me) would have the patience to read the book, except at its high points, more than once. Greig is plainly a gifted and unusual writer, but I hope that his desire to write "really good short lyrics", expressed in an interview in *Verse* with Roderick Watson in 1993, is realised in his next book.

Shirley Geok-lin Lim, a Chinese-American, predominantly writes free verse in conversational rhythms, occasionally using rhyme to bind the whole. There is much talk in the book's introduction (by a professor) of where to "place" her in the English literary canon. Those who don't need to be bothered with such things will turn to the poems and find them the work of a vivacious poet, willing to stuff all sorts of thoughts and feelings into her verse. Many of the poems appear careless on the page, but they would probably work well in performance. They are sometimes engaging, various, hearteningly irreverent and often rather scrappy. So much free verse gathered together makes one realise why the making of formal stanzas is experiencing a resurgence.

I can't read Welsh, and so therefore have to rely, unfairly, on the English translations, by various hands, of Menna Elfyn's *Selected Poems*. These are almost entirely in free verse. Those I like I tend to like in spite of their form, for as translations they are often rhythmically inert: the besetting fault of most modern poetry in English these days, never mind translations. An exception is parts of 'Different Periods' recounting first experiences of menstruation, both by the narrator and (perhaps) a daughter:

I knew when it happened to you. I knew.
What a shy journey we shared, easing
this bout with pure comfort. Then,
I felt I had to celebrate with the dawn-red dew...

How markedly a few rhymes and definite rhythms improve the music of the translation! Still, Elfyn's voice seems genuine, and no doubt only Welsh speakers can appreciate her work at its best. I liked the forthright dignity of the translation of her poem 'Y gneuen wag' ('The Empty Shell'):

> Though my body was not ripe-shelled
> or brown like the fine hazel,
> still, as a young tree I wanted
> to cast nuts for humanity –
> the bite of them hard and true,
> strength the character in their shells.
> But before time, the nut was plucked,
> broken in two inside me;
> nothing but fruit shrivelled
> and despised, thrown back to the river,
> leaving me poverty stricken
> in the midst of splendid hazels.

Gerry Cambridge

Theatre Roundup

I missed a good deal of the official Festival this year, because of relentless footslogging on the Fringe, but must hand it to Brian McMaster for assembling a dazzling array and variety of theatre, with at least three brilliant productions which were unforgettable. First the Citizens' production of *Don Carlos* which I went to not expecting not to enjoy. But it showed the Citizens' at their brilliant best, using all their skill and consummate dramatic artistry with supreme assurance. Robert David MacDonald's translation and Philip Prowse's adaptation of Schiller's masterpiece made it instantly accessible and relevant to a modern audience while retaining the power and poetry of the original. Prowse's set used every inch of space available at the Lyceum: an almost bare stage, framed in a black rectangular box broken only by three doors and dominated above by a huge golden arch, with brilliant simplicity and power suggested all the overweening majesty and despotism of imperial Spain and its king, Philip II, played with utter confidence and regal beauty by Giles Havergal.

This production had the courage of its own arrogance, articulating with eloquence and unapologetic conviction Schiller's great themes about love, betrayal and political power. Benedick Bates lacked range as a too-spluttery Don Carlos, but Andrew Woodall shone as Posa, in a subtle and intelligent performance. It was an uplifting experience to see this supreme achievement of a Scottish company being viewed on an international stage.

Another great Scottish triumph on the Official Festival was TAG's adaptation of Lanark which achieved the near-impossible in the distillation of Alasdair Gray's great and complex novel into a brief two and a half hours. Alastair Cording's adaptation managed to capture the complex inter-relation of different levels of reality and existence captured by the book, supported with pared-down efficiency by Angela Davies's set, in some ways similar to that of *Don Carlos*. The central concept was that the entire play was the creation of the great mural which Duncan Thaw drives himself mad trying to complete. This divine architect was played by a singer, Stuart MacIntyre,

and some of the interlinking of the two main narratives achieved through the music of Alasdair Nicolson. Not everyone liked his very modernistic score, but it more than served its purpose. Nicolson imitated Gray's plagiarisms through musical quotations, many of which remain to be recognised.

The cast had a difficult job to do, and most of them many different roles to perform, and while there wasn't an impressive confidence in the acting, that was made up for by consummate teamwork, and superb performances especially from Tom Smith as Duncan Thaw and Laurance Rudic as Lanark. Oddly enough, both actors, and the singer playing the artist, managed to look curiously like Alasdair Gray himself. Again, to see this ambitious adaptation in the magnificent setting of the Assembly Halls, with its presbyterian austerity, in front of an international audience confirmed the flexibile creativity and vitality of Scottish theatre.

The other great experience of the official festival was *Dans la Solitude des Champs de Coton* by Bernard-Marie Koltes, a remarkable French playwright who died sadly young. *Dans la Solitude* is a Beckett-like masterpiece: two people, a dealer and a client, confront each other in the bleak cavernous setting of the Drill Hall. There ensues a great battle for supremacy, for survival, which, even for those who don't understand the French, quickly assumed metaphysical proportions, becoming a metaphor for the survival of humanity within the exploitative rigours of what might be loosely called the capitalist system. Played with magnetic energy by Patrice Chéreau and Pascal Greggory, these two actors dominate that huge space with their dramatic intensity. There is anothing else there to rely on, no scenery – only a tin can and a coat are used as props – and when the can is kicked you are suddenly faced with the entirety of modern urban squalor; when the coat is dropped on the floor, there is a sound of breaking of glass, as if there is no human comfort to be had anywhere. Yet both the poetic rhythms of Koltes' script and the haunting lilt of a lone woman's singing, which occasionally floats above the protagonists, suggests another reality beyond the dance of death, a life of the spirit, of beauty, rather like that suggested in Louis Macneice's poem 'Prayer before Birth'. The entire audience was rivetted. One of the great privileges of the Edinburgh Festival is to have one's dramatic horizons so enlarged.

The fringe was not so healthy this year. I suspect sheer economics are preventing some of the best productions by small companies coming here at all. I saw a lot of very third-rate Eastern European groups, who failed totally to bridge the language gap in their use of dramatic action. Two plays, however, about Bosnia, stand out. From Poland's Teatre Biuro Podrozy came a brief but outstanding symbolic spectacle, *Carmen Funebre*, performed in the open air at the playground of Drummond Community School. The script, in English, was pared to the bone, but the essence lay in the symbolic orchestration, the scenography and the use of music combined. An inhospitable tower structure looms at one end of the acting area, dimly lit. Suddenly, as if from nowhere, these medieval warlords appear on enormous stilts, helmeted and snapping whips, sometimes stepping right over the heads of the crowd. They pull actors out of the crowd and proceed to pursue them relentlessly around the playground. These symbolic episodes are interrupted with more naturalistic sequences, showing how so many people are corrupted by war.

The company managed to convey so much about the horrors of the war. At one point a washingline is stretched across the area. A woman comes to remove the single white garment it bears, but suddenly garment and rope are wrapped many times around her and there is a terrifying representation of gang-rape by four men, tossing a bottle of crude liquor to each other and laughing cruelly. But there are images of hope also. At one point the actors traverse the length of the area, held in by two long green drapes. They bear lanterns and balloons, which they release, and both lanterns and balloons fly up into the sky and over the roofs of Edinburgh, fading into the distance, but their lights still twinkling like distant stars. It was a stunning dramatic experience.

More than a word must be said too in favour of Allan Sharpe's *Playing Sarajevo*, mounted by Fifth Estate at the Netherbow. The central motif of the play was the magician of Alexander Reid's *The World's Wonder*. Sharpe's intent was at once, in a semi-naturalistic way, to show the incomprehensible complexities of the Bosnian situation, and yet to suggest that art and the imagination are perhaps the only way through to a better existence. Set in a rundown theatre, just taken over as a military hospital, an ageing actor refuses to let go his work, his craft, and a series of other roles; a military doctor, a comotose woman lovingly tended by her husband, a deserter, and others work out a complex plot that acts as a microcosm of the war situation. There's a lot of work still to be done on this play, especially in the second act, but it had real conviction, power, and an electric combination of humour and tragedy. Allan Sharpe gave a heavily powerful performance as the actor, and Alexander West one of the finest and committed showings of his acting career as the doctor. I hope we see a revival of this soon. It deserved more critical acclaim than it got.

Some brief mentions: Edinburgh Theatre Arts gave us a sampling of Robin Lorimer's *Macbeth in Scots*, proving that Shakespeare's English is in fact enriched by the translation into the more elemental and earthy Scots. I was impressed by the energetic, indeed positively health-endangering physical theatre of Pathways Theatre Company with their devised piece *Odyssey*. The National Student Theatre Company play *The North Pole* set in a pub in the north of England was both testingly observed and uncompromisingly performed by a young company, worthy winners of the Guardian Student Theatre Award.

Finally, a look back to spring: more evidence of Robert Lepage's genius with a wonderful Swedish version of Strindberg's *Dream Play* at the Tramway. Kenny Ireland vindicated his enthusiasm for Howard Barker with his stark but unforgettable production of *The Castle*. By comparison, David Mamet's *Oleanna* proved itself a shallow failure in its attempt to deal with the theme of political correctness. The Lyceum itself is showing brilliant colours lately, especially in its exuberant and bouncy production of *Loot*, and, surprise surprise, a stylish and almost faultless version of Coward's *Private Lives* which reminded us all of just how good and profound a playwright Coward is.   *Joy Hendry*

Pamphleteer

Have you ever fallen in love with a book cover? *The Tides in the Basin* by Patricia Pogson (Flambard Press, 4 Mitchell Avenue, Jesmond, Newcastle NE2 3LA, £6.95) has an attractive front but even better is the geometric design on *The Violet Room* by Julie Whitby (Acumen, 6 The Mount, Higher Furzeham, Brixham, S Devon TQ5 8QY, £4.25). Pogson is an award-winning poet who in her own calm way points to happenings in various parts of the globe, and invites us clearly to take a look. With Whitby, one cannot help but be impressed by the sweep of her emotions. Her poem based around Pisarro's *The Road in Louveciennes* is quite unique.

A large softbound pamphlet with colourful illustrations is *Sandy and the Spoot Boots* from Peedie Broon Publications of Stromness (£5.95). It is an Orcadian tale full of fun and let us see more of the same, please.

The first of a planned series from Pikestaff Press is *First Selection* by Robert Roberts. Robert sets many of his poems around the Otter Valley, Devon. Two words can accurately describe his poems: well-crafted. Here are lines of verse that carry you along with ease, as seen in 'Local Heaven':

It was but yesterday – to force our scene
Into sharp contrast – that, beneath black skies
Thrown across Exmoor from the west, we'd been
Striding the Quantocks, shoulderings that rise
Above all Somerset, it seemed, to where
The Welsh hills lour and black seas flow between

Here is poetry free of the stresses of inner-city life, and very much alive. This book is recommended to those who appreciate fine verse. Obtainable from Pikestaff Press, Ellon House, Harpford, Sidmouth, Devon EX10 0NH (£2.00)

Raunchland Publications, 2 Henderson St, Kingseat, Dunfermline KY12 0TP has *The Riddle of Pain* (£2) with three poets from North-east England. If your idea of a poem is 13 words on 6 lines, then see 'Unmoved' by Adam Sykes. Derek Woodcock writes faithfully on graft inside a factory, and Tom Kelly touches on hard life in the suburbs.

To North-east Scotland now and the booklet *Ah wish Ah hid a fiver* by Marjory Nicholson (published by Banff & Buchan District Council, £1.50). For me, the poems written in her own spik stand out. And it is refreshing to see poems which speak of modern-day things, like the Child Support Agency, within a poem in Scots.

Two publications from Spout, Birstall Library, Market Street, Birstall, Batley, West Yorkshire WF17 9EN – *You What* by John Bosley and *Piltdown Man and Bat Woman* by Milner Place, both £2.50. John Bosley rarely uses rhyme, lines of equal length, or commas. This is different to the poetry of, for example, Robert Roberts. Yet in his poem 'And before that' John can achieve a magical effect. The poem itself is about an old couple at work in their garden and the lines quoted below appear towards the end. The magic is in the final line, which is here withheld:

> There had been railway wagons
> cranes and piles of coal
> changes, worries, accidents
> debts and threats from oil;
> and before that the war.

Milner Place is plainly following his own style and shows some intriguing phrases – "...while the jukebox drummed out the rhythm of chains", "...see how mist on a morning river cons time".

And three publications from Smith/Doorstep Books, The Studio, Byram Arcade, Westgate, Huddersfield HD1 1ND, all at £2.95. *icefall climbing* by Pascale Petit, who trained as a sculptor, *be prepared* by Peter Daniels, who trained as a librarian and indexer, and *young men dancing* by Linda Chase, who teaches Tai Chi. If P Petit writes poetry then I am a platypus. The longer poems on the mountains of Tibet and Brazil are prose. P Daniels has poems on Inchcolm, Palermo, New York in the good ole USA, Birmingham in the UK, and an interplanetary poem on butches and femmes converging on Earthlings. L Chase manages to entertain and goodness me! Do I see an overt referral to sexual activity in the poem 'What's a Shirt Between Friends?':

Hey! My jeans are white. I don't want dirt on them, I'll slip them slightly past the slot.

Cliff Forshaw's *Strange Tongues* has poems and translations, and his *Minus Twenty-seven* has three poems for a Russian

New Year, both books by Weasel Productions, 29 Appach Road, London SW2 2LD, priced £3.50 and £2 respectively. We are lucky that Cliff had been a traveller and not a couch potato. His tone is dauntless, the language vigorous; he jolts, cuts, whips, flicks, plunges in the appropriate place. In 'Through The Forest' he does not need to say it is wintertime in Russia... the poem begins:

Minus twenty seven. The town gives out,
trolleybuses terminate in dirty snow.
Out there it's clean. You click skis...

Click, Crackle, Spassky, Sparkle – his poetry is loud with noise and crammed with eerie sights. My advice? Buy! Buy!

Big Little Poem Books, 3 Park Avenue, Melton Mowbray, Leicestershire LE13 0JB have Shirley Bell, Sarah Lawson, Vicki Raymond and Julie Whitby in *Outside the Chain of Hands* (£3.90). Vicki Raymond who writes sharply and Julie Whitby who is more lyrical, use rhyme occasionally, but why are there not more rhyming poems throughout? The poems of S Bell and S Lawson are in 'modern style' and the subject matter of 'Dog-days', 'Soft Fruits', 'Mexico City College', 'Twiddling the Wheel', dare I say it, seem to lack vitality. If such poetry is seen as a reflection of the sweet, nice Nineties, fair enough.

George Cameron aspires to make the life of Wick-born John Horne (1861–1934) better known, hence his 137-page book *John Horne, His Life and Works*. A pastor in Glasgow, John Horne was later a businessman in Ayr, and an author, one volume being *Caithnessian Poems and Plays* (1923). The events of his life, and early photographs, are published by North of Scotland Newspapers, 42 Union Street, Wick. The book has much material of social interest, on the charms of Caithness, and though written in the English I see among the reminiscences section this line, set in the hills of Knockdry at Ulbster:

A schochad passing overhead throws its shadow on the green spots, almost as definitely as his body shows against the sky.

...after extensive enquiry, just what a schochad was remains a mystery. That it was not a Tornado jet on a training flight is certain.

Improvisations by Jay Ramsay is a sequence of nine long poems, recorded direct on a Walkman while on the sands of Traeth near Portmadog. Available from Stride, 11 Sylvan Road, Exeter EX4 6EW (£6.50). Ramsay can write on landscape, nature and human beings though this is not uncommon among poets. And other poets who can write free of rentagob rant are not unknown. Cast as a spiritual poem *Improvisations* might appeal to some who find the Morning of the Wise, the daughters of God, the Lord of the Ether, the Sister of Gold and Brother of Daylight of interest.

Two essays are together in a pamphlet from Neruda Press, 51 Allison Street, Glasgow G42 8NG, *the Hegemony of Ideas* and *Mental Asylums and the Looney Left* (£1) The two brave authors are Dermot and Paul Anderson.

Three Nights in Perthshire has a foreword by Margaret, the Lady Thatcher. We are assured that the former Prime Minister is familiar with the present-day farm of Ledard including its special goats – we understand that these are four-legged ruminants who produce cashmere wool. The book is in fact a new edition of a book of the same title written by a young Glasgow bookseller, Thomas Atkinson, in 1821. Further, Atkinson's account of his visit to the Trossachs can be seen as a forerunner to Stevenson's *Inland Voyage*. The lands of Ladarde, the annual Hairst Kirn, local ballads and songs and battles are all featured in this handsome book with its cover of a pastoral watercolour. Published by Creag Darach, Milton of Aberfoyle, Stirling FK8 3TD, £3.95.

Watch out! The ladies and gentlemen of the Johnstone Writers' Group will not stop writing short stories and poetry. *Glimpsed Edges* is the title of their sixth anthology, and good stuff it is too. The three poems by Robert Lauder have caught my eye. Robert says in one, "look at him, he thinks he is the height of fashion" about the groom wearing the skirt, earrings and the ponytail. Another poem 'One Eye' about a child's missing teddy-bear, is a delight. A first inclusion for Janice Grant with 'The Govanettes', a short story of two schoolgirls, which I like very much. The dialogue is authentic, the plot is not over-elaborated, and the plot moves smoothly. Watch out Catherine Cookson! For a copy of *Glimpsed Edges* send £2 to Jack Hastie, Dunadd, Lewis Crescent, Kilbarchan PA10 2HB.   *Brent Hodgson*

Catalogue

After Canongate's recent adventures with the Albany Book Company, and other optimistic beginnings among Scottish publishers that have fallen into difficulty, a large pile of books from a new or newish publisher invites mixed emotions. Delight that another swells the ranks; concern that the star should not burn too bright and fade too soon – especially with the Net Book Agreement falling apart. But let's welcome B&W's enterprise. They've been around for a while already, making their name particularly with Scots texts, notably *A Tongue In Yer Heid*. This radical expansion of their catalogue is achieved with a blend of classics, back-catalogue reprints, and new titles, cumulatively inventing a history for the company. Which are classics and which back-catalogue can be debated, but the titles include Neil Munro's *The New Road* (£6.99), John Buchan's *The Free Fishers* and *John Burnet of Barns* (both £5.99), Guy McCrone's *Aunt Bel* – surely a candidate for serialisation on the telly – (£5.99), *Scenes and Legends of the North of Scotland* by Hugh Miller, a kind of Doric James Hogg (£8.99) – (pause for breath) – *Lion Rampant*, Robert Woollcombe's personal reminiscences of World War II (£7.99), *The Tobacco Lords Trilogy* of Margaret Thomson Davis, set in Glasgow during the 1745 Rising (£7.99), Nigel Tranter's historical novels *Tinker's Pride* and *Fast & Loose* (both £5.99); finally, two volumes of Jack Webster, former editor of the *Scottish Daily Express*: *Grains of Truth* (£7.99) is his two volumes of autobiography (*A Grain of Truth* and – yes – *Another Grain of Truth*) collected in one volume, while *The Express Years: A Golden Decade* is a collection of articles first published during the 1960s. (B&W Publishing, 7 Sciennes, Edinburgh, EH9 1NH)

Following his immensely valuable *Scottish Art 1460–1990*, Duncan Macmillan turns his unrivalled expertise to *Scottish Art in the 20th Century* (Mainstream, £20). A lot of superlatives for one sentence, but fully merited. Mainstream does excellent service to Scottish fine art, even if John McEwen's *John Bellany* (£30) breezes through the master's life and times with a cheeriness at odds with some of the paintings illustrated.

Among Islands (Mainstream, £14.99) sees Jim Crumley navigating the islands north and west of mainland Scotland and writing warmly, if that is the word, of his journey. *In Search of Tusitala* is a similar kind of book, being Gavin Bell's account of his following of R L Stevenson's route through the Pacific (Picador, £15.99). Unfortunately, the dynamics don't work: Bell, as an experienced war correspondent, is on sabbatical where Stevenson was adventuring *in extremis*. From John Donald (£8.95) comes *Discovering the Borders* by Alan Spence (the one without the spectacles), an agreeable guide to the Borders heartland around Tweeddale. *The Last Hundred: Munros, Beards and a Dog* needs little elaboration, being a book about ascending Munros with a dog by a man with a beard, namely Hamish Brown (Mainstream, £14.99). The dug, needless to say, steals the show. What an extraordinary variety of mottoes have the Scottish families listed in the *Scottish Clan and Family Encyclopaedia* (George Way & Romilly Squire, Collins, £25), the pompous, the pious, the enigmatic, the dry, the unarguable ("Either peace or war", Gunn); all that, brief histories, and family tartans too. *Scotland: The Land and the Whisky* (Roddy Martine & Patrick Douglas Hamilton, John Murray, £29.95) raises the interesting sociological question, do the people who go shootin' up north have coffee tables? For these seem to be the people for whom the book is intended.

Ronald Stevenson belongs in a tradition of European music that took a completely different line to the mainstream who followed Liszt and Wagner through to Schoenberg, serialism and beyond. Instead the line went from Liszt to Busoni and other specialist composers for the piano, through the likes of Medtner and Sorabji; and at present Stevenson is as prominent an inheritor as any. His recent *A Child's Garden of Verses* has been published by the Ronald Stevenson Society (3 Chamberlain Road, Edinburgh EH10 4DL) – a setting of Robert Louis Stevenson's poems commissioned by the BBC for the volume's centenary in 1985. As Stevenson has taken the adult approach to the poetry, the settings exhibit his customary facility with the piano, but are by no means easy to play, giving an impression of childhood rather than an imitation of it. There is an accompanying volume, an analysis and commentary by Colin Scott-Sutherland, available from the Society.

Passing the subject of childhood, in some senses a lost childhood too, the Pelican Publishing Company (1101 Monroe St, PO Box 3110, Gretna, LA70053) has *The Wee Scot Book* by Aileen Campbell, a collection of Scottish folk tales illustrated in colour, aimed at young children living outside Scotland . It manages very well to avoid the misty-eyed sentimentalist approach, and Pelican have a range of further titles of interest to Scots in America and American Scots. The Master, meanwhile, has another volume out: Stanley Robertson's *Ghosties and Ghoulies* (Balnain, £6.99) is a spell-binding and not too chilling collection of eldritch tales. From Polygon comes a slightly over-designed overview of storytelling in *Scottish Traditional Tales*, edited by the sadly late Alan Bruford and Donald MacDonald. All that such a volume can – or should – do is give as full an impression as space allows of the historical context and the contemporary breadth and depth of resource, drawing together regions and cultures to suggest a whole. It will never be comprehensive: that is something time's passing doesn't allow. But this book does a superb job, not least in attempting to notate the sound of the voice along with the story.

The Oxford Guide to British Women Writers (Joanne Shattock, OUP, £7.99) tends to be more reliable on historical names. It's always easy to pick holes in this kind of book, but Carol Ann Duffy, Jackie Kay seem glaring omissions given the presence of contemporaries. Francis Hutcheson's philosophy influenced both Hume and Adam Smith. His *Philosophical Writings* are well worth Everyman's £6.99 both for the thought and for the between-the-lines views on other thinkers. I was thinking, this is a crap story, as I was reading Brian McCabe's 'Story Report' in *The Bridport Prize* anthology, how on earth did it win? Then I realised that it was a report. The anthology is published every year, and the prize is one of this island's most important. (Redcliff Press/Bridport Arts Centre, South Street, Bridport, Dorset, £4.99). *The Return of Burke and Hare* (Dualchas, £4.99) is a play by Raymond Burke with an entertaining intro-

duction by Owen Dudley Edwards, himself the author of a Burke and Hare play. Don't be deceived: this is a satire on the modern health service, and not in the best possible taste.

It doesn't take many sentences of *The Smile of the Unknown Mariner* (Vincenzo Consolo, Carcanet, £14.95) to realise this is a novel of the highest quality, rich, beautiful and deeply imaginative in its language, sympathetically translated by Joseph Farrell. It's set in Sicily, 1860, in the company of Garibaldi, but beyond that impossible to summarise. *Storm 6: Out of Yugoslavia* (Carcanet, £7.95) is an anthology searching for identity among bloody and tattered remains. Perhaps the filtering implicit in publishing these *particular* writers isn't helpful, as it is presumably a judgement made from outside, but in a sense it is the least hopeless place to start looking for a solution. *S.E. Asia Writes Back!* (Skoob Pacifica Anthology No. 1, £5.99) is worth the admission money for three essays by Nobel Laureates Walcott, Soyinka and Kabawata addressing the identity issue, never mind the high-quality new writing sandwiching them.

Poem for the Day, ed Nicholas Albery (Sinclair Stevenson, £9.99) includes amusing and brief comments on each poem in this widenetted anthology. An ideal dipping book, as is *The Routledge Anthology of Poets on Poets*, ed David Hopkins, ranging from Auden's touching 'In Memory of W B Yeats' to Dryden's savagely funny 'Flecknoe Celebrates Shadwell's Talents'. Well-indexed though bad for footnotes (ie too many).

From Bloodaxe, *The Ice Pilot Speaks* by Pauline Stainer: images floating densely in front of your eyes like a snowfall, with shortbreathed rhythms suggestive of Emily Dickinson. Linda France, in *The Gentleness of the Very Tall* is bolder, more boisterous in her use of language and rhythm. Geoff Hattersley, in *Don't Worry*, has an aggressive, witty voice with a transatlantic twang, and, it's worth noting, an eye for his immediate surroundings more usually associated with women writers. Douglas Houston dispenses imagery with more formal pacing, rich with allusion, as in 'Encounter': "I met Breugel in a pub last night/ On an ageing Birmingham council estate". I especially enjoyed 'Nicotinic Sonnet', even though I've given up.

Notes on Contributors

Leila Aboulela: Egyptian/Sudanese, born 1964, came from Sudan seven years ago to study Statistics at London School of Economics. Now lives in Aberdeen with her family and teaches part time.

Angus Calder: writer who lives in Edinburgh, tired of being best known as the author of *The People's War* – aspiring minor poet!

Gerry Cambridge: born 1959, poet, former freelance journalist and photographer; editor of *The Dark Horse* magazine.

Patrick Clark: retired teacher, winner of the *Spectator/ Johnnie Walker Poetry Prize* in 1984. Now 73, he has waited patiently for two years for these poems to appear in *Chapman*!

Peter Cudmore: currently on Cultural Policy and Management course at Moray House, still helping out with *Chapman* from time to time.

Christine De Luca: born & brought up in Shetland. Former teacher, now educational researcher. First poetry collection, *Voes and Sounds*, written in Shetlandic & English, published by Shetland Library.

John Dixon: the nice man who gave the editor a first edition of an early volume of William Soutar's poetry! At present completing his own second collection, the first being *Scots Baronial* (Polygon).

Alec Finlay: writer, editor and publisher of Morning Star Publications, currently editing Hamish Henderson's *Collected Works* for Polygon of which *Alias MacAlias* (Essays) appeared in 1992. *The Armstrong Nose* (Selected Letters) will appear soon.

William Graham: born Carluke 1913; lived, until his death last year, in Alloway. Educated at Glasgow University, he was an organist, nurseryman, airman, teacher and author. Published work includes *That Ye Inherit*, the seminal *Scots Word Book*, 1977 and *October Sunset*, his last book of poems and stories. Founder member and Honorary Vice-Preses of the Scots Language Society.

C. M. Grieve: aka Hugh MacDiarmid, great poet and controversialist of 20th century Scottish cultural life.

Hamish Henderson: poet, folklorist (never retired) at the School of Scottish Studies, prime mover behind the Scottish Folk Revival, and legend in his own time.

Brent Hodgson: New Zealand-born writer of fiction and poetry. Likes words and the Old Scots language. Awarded an SAC writer's bursary 1995. Has travelled widely encouraging Scottish sheep to write poetry.

Robert Alan Jamieson: born Shetland, currently William Soutar Fellow, living in Soutar Hoose in Perth, poet, novelist and co-editor of *The Edinburgh Review*.

Norman Kreitman lives in Edinburgh and recently retired from research in psychiatry, now struggling with a book on aesthetics. His poetry includes *Touching Rock* (1987) and *Against Leviathan* (1989) both published by the Aberdeen University Press. A third collection is in preparation.

Ian McDonough: born in Brora, Sutherland, community worker, member of Edinburgh's Shore Poets and represented in their recent anthology, *The Golden Goose Hour*.

Elise McKay: teacher, now retired, has appeared in several poetry magazines and had two collections of poetry published, *Unravelling Sheets* (Outposts) and *Floating Lanterns* (Envoi).

Issy McKnight: devoted grandmother, she worked as a clerk before graduating from Dundee University and going into social work. She wrote these poems following the end of her 30 year marriage.

Deborah Moffatt: born 1953, Vermont, USA, lives in Fife, received a Scottish Arts Council Bursary in 1986. Her stories and poems have appeared in a number of publications, including *Acumen, Verse, Cosmopolitan, Soho Square* and Faber's *First Fictions*.

Catriona Newman: new writer, part-time artist. Soon to be mother of six. Placed in recent national poetry competition.

John Purser: chief moving spirit behind *Scotland's Music*. Has published poetry and written a number of radio plays, including *Parrots and Owls* and the award-winning *Carver*. He is currently working on a new play, *The Secret Commonwealth*, for Radio 3.

Kathleen Raine: poet, editor and Blake scholar, editor of the magazine *Temenos* and founder of The Temenos Foundation in London – a long-standing friend of Tom Scott.

David Summers lives in Edinburgh and works as a lecturer.

Billy Watt: born in Greenock and now Principal Teacher of English at Broxburn Academy. He writes fiction and poetry.